CW00434932

UNDERSTANDING THE DISCIPLINE OF
FASTING

PAUL DAVID WASHER

"Fasting is an important biblical discipline for private and public devotion. Yet it is generally forgotten today, as if it were part of some extreme asceticism that we have outgrown. In this much-needed workbook, Paul Washer leads us through a thoughtful, thorough, and helpful study of the Holy Scriptures to show us how to practice fasting according to God's revealed will. I pray that God will use this study mightily to restore the spiritual discipline of fasting to its rightful place in many thousands of Christian lives."

— Dr. Joel R. Beeke, President of Puritan Reformed Theological Seminary

"It was my pleasure and privilege to be introduced to this workbook! Unfortunately, fasting has become unpopular or simply uncomfortable to many churches, despite the wealth of spiritual benefit and blessing that can be enjoyed if it is properly understood. This book does a masterful job of providing a comprehensive study of the subject and doing so in a way that is carefully balanced to avoid the errors and excesses that sometimes accompany such practices. I thank God for leading me to this precious work for my own personal benefit, and I heartily recommend it to every child of God seeking to take his or her Christian walk seriously and soberly."

— Steven Lee, Founder of SermonAudio

"In His most famous sermon, Jesus Christ said to His disciples, 'When ye fast,' assuming their practice of that discipline. However, many in our day assume that fasting was laid in the tomb with our Savior and did not come out with Him. Paul Washer examines that erroneous thinking by the burning light of Holy Scripture; the result is the most biblical, concise, and useful handbook on the discipline of fasting I have read. The heart and soul of this book is about laying hold of holy, ardent, Spirit-transformed Christian living, aided by the discipline of fasting. Study it prayerfully, apply it carefully, and live it wholeheartedly for the glory of Christ. You cannot do so without profiting your soul."

— Jeff Pollard, Pastor of Mt. Zion Bible Church and Editor of Free Grace Broadcaster

UNDERSTANDING THE DISCIPLINE OF **FASTING**

Copyright 2023 Paul David Washer

All rights reserved. No part of this book may be used or reproduced in any manner whatsoever without written permission except in the case of brief quotations embodied in critical articles and reviews. Direct your requests to the publisher at the following address.

Published by:

HeartCry Missionary Society
PO Box 7372
Roanoke, VA 24019

www.heartcrymissionary.com

Printed in the United States of America 2023
Second Edition, Second Printing

Unless otherwise noted, all Scripture quotations taken from the
New American Standard Bible®
Copyright 1960, 1962, 1963, 1968, 1971, 1972, 1973, 1975, 1977, 1995
by the Lockman Foundation. Used by permission.

Edited by Meghan Nash and Forrest Hite
Additional proofreading by Mary Claire Castleberry and Joel Kady
Layout and design by Jon Green, Matthew Robinson, Forrest Hite, and Michael Reece

Table of Contents

UNDERSTANDING THE DISCIPLINE OF FASTING

Introduction

METHOD OF STUDY

The great goal of this study is for the student to have an encounter with God through His Word. Founded upon the conviction that the Scriptures are the inspired and infallible Word of God, this study has been designed in such a way that it is literally impossible for the student to advance without an open Bible before him or her. The goal is to help the reader obey the exhortation of the Apostle Paul in II Timothy 2:15:

> *Be diligent to present yourself approved to God as a workman who does not need to be ashamed, accurately handling the word of truth.*

Each chapter deals with a specific aspect of the discipline of fasting or the solemn assembly. The student will complete each chapter by answering the questions and following the instructions according to the Scriptures given. The student is encouraged to meditate upon each text and write his or her thoughts. The benefit gained from this study will depend upon the student's investment. If the student answers the questions thoughtlessly, merely copying the text without seeking to understand its meaning, this book will be of very little help.

Understanding the Discipline of Fasting is primarily a biblical study and does not contain much in the way of colorful illustrations, quaint stories, or theological treatises. It was the desire of the author to provide a work that simply points the way to the Scriptures and allows the Word of God to speak for itself.

This workbook may be used by an individual, in a small group, for a Sunday school class, or in other contexts. It is highly recommended that the student complete each chapter on his or her own before meeting for discussion and questions with a group or discipleship leader.

EXHORTATION TO THE STUDENT

The student is encouraged to study biblical doctrine and discover its exalted place in the Christian life. The true Christian cannot bear or even survive a divorce between the emotions and the intellect or between devotion to God and the doctrine of God. According to the Scriptures, neither our emotions nor our experiences provide an adequate foundation for the Christian life. Only the truths of Scripture, understood with the mind and communicated through doctrine, can provide that sure foundation upon which we should establish our beliefs and our behavior and determine the validity of our emotions and experiences. The mind is not the enemy of the heart, and doctrine is not an obstacle to devotion. The two are indispensable and should be inseparable. The Scriptures command us to love the Lord our God with all our heart, with all our soul, and with all our mind (Matthew 22:37) and to worship God both in spirit and in truth (John 4:24).

The study of doctrine is both an intellectual and devotional discipline. It is a passionate search for God that should always lead the student to greater personal transformation, obedience, and heartfelt worship. Therefore, the student should be on guard against the great error of seeking only impersonal knowledge instead of the person of God. Neither mindless devotion nor mere intellectual pursuits are profitable, for in either case, God is lost.

THE NEW AMERICAN STANDARD BIBLE

The New American Standard Bible (1995 edition) is required to complete this study. This version of Scripture was chosen for the following reasons: (1) the unwavering conviction of its translators that the Bible is the infallible Word of God; and (2) its faithfulness to the original languages.

A WORD FROM THE AUTHOR

To claim to be an expert in even the most minor subjects touching the Scriptures betrays both arrogance and ignorance. This is especially true with regard to the private devotions of Bible reading, prayer, and fasting. I have yet to meet a man who lamented spending too much time in these devotions, yet I have known countless men (including myself) who lament their all-to-frequent neglect. Are we not all prone to identify with Martha who was "worried and bothered about so many things," while neglecting the "good part" that was chosen by Mary (Luke 10:41-42)?

Having given the above disclaimer, I can now move on to my motive or reason for writing this workbook on fasting. It is threefold. First, I write because the discipline of fasting is a biblical devotion that was practiced in both the Old and New Testaments. Second, I write because so many believers, young and old, have questioned me through the years regarding its proper place in the Christian life and about how it ought to be practiced. Finally, I write because there is so little information available on the subject.

It is a good thing that the people of God still count Bible study and prayer as foundational disciplines of the Christian life and consider those who are faithful in these disciplines to be noble and wise. At the same time, it is lamentable that so many contemporary Christians have very wrong views of fasting—whether that is a relic of the past; that it is an impossible feat to be practiced by only the spiritually elite; or (worst of all) that it is a harmful ritual practiced by only the most severe fanatics, who believe that the destruction of the body is the only road to true holiness. I have written this workbook to expose these erroneous ideas and to help the people of God to understand the discipline of fasting and its proper place in the Christian life.

To conclude, I would like to thank my wife Charo for her timely encouragement in every endeavor and my four children (Ian, Evan, Rowan, and Bronwyn), who continue to be a great blessing. I would also like to thank HeartCry staff member Forrest Hite for his editing of the manuscript and his supervision over the graphics, layout, and design. His contributions to the overall readability of this work were invaluable. My thanks are also extended to the entire HeartCry staff. They have been a great encouragement throughout the process of this book's writing and publication.

A WORD FROM THE EDITOR

Included at the end of this book is a brief work by Thomas Boston, a Scottish theologian greatly respected by both the author (Paul Washer) and the editor (myself, Forrest Hite). *Personal Fasting and Humiliation* is an abridged and modernized version of *A Memorial Concerning Personal and Family Fasting and Humiliation*, which itself was published in Boston's *Whole Works (Volume 11)*.

There are relatively few works that deal with the topic of fasting, so it was hard for us to find books for students to advance their study on the discipline. We decided to include Boston's brief writing on the subject in part to help alleviate this problem—especially since it was previously difficult to access, buried within Boston's *Whole Works*. We hope that bringing this older work back to light will prove to be a blessing for many.

Once the decision was made to include *Personal Fasting and Humiliation*, we felt it necessary to consider its readership. Paul Washer's *Understanding the Discipline of Fasting*, as with all of his workbooks in the Biblical Foundations for the Christian Faith series, was written to be as understandable as possible to the student, whatever his or her background. Boston, on the other hand, penned his treatise in the early 18th century; much of the language used then is currently rather difficult to understand.

Therefore, I undertook the process of abridgement and modernization in order to emphasize clarity, simplifying the language as much as possible without weakening the meaning. Indeed, much care was taken to minimize the changes and to be true to the author's intent. Where more significant edits were necessary to clarify the meaning, I have included footnotes of the book's original verbiage for those phrases or sentences to ensure that Boston's words are not misconstrued—and also at times to give a glimpse of the beauty of some of the older language.

I added a few reflective questions at the end of each of the three included chapters in order to allow the student room to write his or her thoughts and to continue the workbook format. I pray and trust that *Personal Fasting and Humiliation* will prove helpful and edifying for everyone who works through *Understanding the Discipline of Fasting*.

RECOMMENDED RESOURCES FOR FURTHER STUDIES

Sanctify the Congregation by Richard Owen Roberts (and others)
Personal Fasting and Humiliation by Thomas Boston (included)
"A Desperate Case—How to Meet It" [sermon] by Charles H. Spurgeon
Sermons 98 and 99: The Duty, the Benefits, and the Proper Method of Religious Fasting by Samuel Miller
The Doctrine of Fasting and Prayer and Humiliation for Sin by Arthur Hildersham (for advanced students)

ADDITIONAL NOTE

You may have noticed that this book is being sold at a strange price. Here's why: one dollar ($) from every copy sold will go directly to fund mission work through HeartCry Missionary Society (heartcrymissionary.com). The rest of the sale price is just enough to cover the cost of printing, publication, and distribution. The author is not profiting from the sale of this book, nor has he profited from the sale of any other book. Over the years, we have utilized and explored many avenues in order to publish these workbooks. Ultimately, we have reached the conclusion that doing so in-house at a low cost, even with slightly lower quality, is the most effective way of getting these useful tools into the hands of as many people across the globe as possible. We hope and pray that the Lord continues to use these books to point His people to His Word unto the edification of His church.

Optional Study Schedule

UNDERSTANDING THE DISCIPLINE OF FASTING

Week One: Introduction to Fasting & Fasting Upward
Day 1:   Chapter 1
Day 2:   Chapter 2
Day 3:   Chapter 3
Day 4:   Chapter 4
Day 5:   Chapter 5

Week Two: Fasting Inward
Day 1:   Chapter 6, Section 1
          Chapter 6, Section 2, Main Point 1
Day 2:   Chapter 6, Section 2, Main Points 2-4
Day 3:   Chapter 7
Day 4:   Chapter 8
Day 5:   Prayerful Review

Week Three: Fasting Outward & The Solemn Assembly
Day 1:   Chapter 9, Section 1
          Chapter 9, Section 2
          Chapter 9, Section 3, Main Points 1-2
Day 2:   Chapter 9, Section 3, Main Points 3-5
          Chapter 9, Section 4
Day 3:   Chapter 10
          Chapter 11, Section 1, Main Points 1-2
Day 4:   Chapter 11, Section 1, Main Points 3-7
Day 5:   Chapter 11, Section 2
          Chapter 12

Week Four: Biblical Directions Concerning Fasting
Day 1:   Chapter 13, Section 1
Day 2:   Chapter 13, Sections 2-3
Day 3:   Chapter 14
Day 4:   Appendix
Day 5:   Prayerful Review

PERSONAL FASTING AND HUMILIATION

Week Five: Personal Fasting and Humiliation

Chapter 1: Introduction to Fasting

WHAT IS FASTING?

Throughout the Scriptures, fasting is associated mostly with abstaining from food for a specific period of time for the purpose of seeking God. The fundamental principle of fasting may also include abstinence from any activity, event, or temporal pleasure for the sake of drawing near to God—abstaining from companionship to spend time alone with God; abstaining from sleep to pass the night in prayer; or abstaining from a certain labor, hobby, or pastime to dedicate time to God.

BIBLICAL EXAMPLES OF FASTING

The following is a fairly comprehensive list of Scriptural references to fasting. Included are texts that relate only indirectly to fasting, such as those referring to a hunger or thirst for God. Thoughtfully and prayerfully review this list.

Leviticus 16:29, 31: On the Day of Atonement, the people of Israel were commanded to humble or afflict their souls. This phrase expresses self-denial and is connected most often with fasting (Psalm 35:13; Isaiah 58:3; Ezra 8:21). See also Leviticus 23:27-29 and Acts 27:9.

Exodus 24:12-18: Moses fasted on Mount Sinai forty days and nights while receiving the stone tablets of the Law (Deuteronomy 9:9).

Exodus 34:27-28: Moses fasted on Mount Sinai for forty days and nights to intercede for rebellious Israel and to receive a second copy of the Law (Deuteronomy 9:17-19; 10:10).

Judges 20:26-28: Israel fasted and inquired of the Lord for direction in the war against the tribe of Benjamin.

I Samuel 1:6-11: Hannah fasted and prayed for God to open her womb and give her a son.

I Samuel 7:6-8: Israel fasted in repentance at Mizpah and asked the Lord for deliverance.

I Samuel 31:11-13: The valiant men of Jabesh-gilead fasted in mourning for the death and desecration of King Saul and his sons.

II Samuel 1:11-12: David and his men fasted in mourning for the death of Saul, Jonathan, and those who had fallen by the sword in the battle against the Philistines.

II Samuel 12:15-23: David fasted that God might show mercy and spare the life of his child whom God had struck terminally ill as judgment.

I Kings 21:9-13: Jezebel and Ahab used fasting to feign piety toward God and to mask their plot to kill Naboth.

I Kings 21:20-29: After hearing God's judgment upon him through Elijah, King Ahab humbled himself before God through fasting.

II Chronicles 20:1-4: King Jehoshaphat and Judah fasted to be delivered from the threat of war from the Moabites, Ammonites, and Meunites.

Ezra 8:21-23: Ezra and the exiles with him humbled themselves with fasting that God might give them a safe journey from the river of Ahava to Jerusalem.

Nehemiah 1:3-11; 2:1-8: Nehemiah fasted in mourning over the remnant in Jerusalem who were greatly distressed and under reproach, in confession of the sins of Israel, and in petition of God for mercy and for favor in the eyes of King Artaxerxes.

Nehemiah 8:18; 9:1-3: Israel fasted in a solemn assembly to hear the Law of God and to confess their sins and the sins of their fathers.

Esther 4:16: Queen Esther, her maidens, and the Jews in Susa fasted that she might find favor before the king and that the Jews might be delivered from the destruction that Haman had plotted.

Esther 9:20-22, 30-31: The day of Purim was established as a holiday in commemoration of the Jews' great deliverance from the decrees of Haman and all their enemies. The celebration included not only feasting and rejoicing and gift-giving, but also fasting and lamentation.

Psalm 4:7: God brings greater gladness to the heart than grain and new wine.

Psalm 34:8: David admonished God's people to taste and see for themselves that the Lord is good.

Psalm 35:13-14: David humbled his soul with fasting before God for the sake of others when they were sick and needy.

Psalm 42:1-2; 63:1: The psalmist described a passion for God as a hunger and thirst for Him.

Psalm 69:9-10: David wept and fasted because of his zeal for the things of God and because of the godless who reproached God's name.

Psalm 27:4: David's greatest desire was to behold God's beauty.

Psalm 73:25: Asaph desired nothing on the earth above God and His presence.

Psalm 102:4; 107:18: God's people were represented as being so afflicted that they were said to "forget" (102:4) or even "abhor" their food (107:18).

Psalm 109:24: David was physically weakened from fasting in the midst of his enemies.

Isaiah 58:1-5: Israel asked why God had not noticed their fasts. God rebuked them for their wickedness and hypocrisy.

Isaiah 58:6-14: God described the fasts performed by the righteous that are pleasing to Him.

Jeremiah 36:9-10; 36:20-26: All the people from Jerusalem and the cities of Judah proclaimed a fast and listened as the scroll of Jeremiah was read; however, God's warning was not heeded.

Daniel 6:16-19: King Darius spent the night fasting for the deliverance of Daniel, whom he had unwittingly condemned to the lions' den.

Daniel 9:3-20: Daniel fasted as he confessed his sin and the sin of his people.

Daniel 9:2; 22-23: Daniel fasted as he asked for wisdom to understand the prophecies concerning Israel's future.

Joel 1:14-15; 2:12-17: God commanded Israel to fast and call a solemn assembly in order to repent and plead for mercy before the coming of the day of the Lord (God's judgment).

Jonah 3:4-10: After the preaching of Jonah, the Ninevites called a fast, repented of their wickedness, and pleaded that the Lord would be merciful.

Zechariah 7:1-7; 8:19: During their exile, the Jews established four annual fasts: one each in the fourth, fifth, seventh, and tenth months.

Matthew 4:1-3: Jesus fasted for forty days and nights in the wilderness prior to being tested by the tempter.

Matthew 6:16: Jesus assumed that fasting would be practiced by His disciples and warned against improper motives (*e.g.* hypocrisy) when fasting.

Matthew 6:17-18: Jesus taught about the proper motives for fasting and the promise of reward.

Matthew 9:14-15: Jesus taught that His disciples would fast after His ascension.

Matthew 9:16-17: Jesus distinguished between the old order of fasting, which was practiced by the Pharisees and the disciples of John the Baptist, and the new order of fasting, which would be practiced by His disciples.

Mark 9:29: Jesus mentioned fasting along with prayer as a means of strengthening the believer's faith for spiritual warfare. *Variations in translation related to this text are discussed in the next section.*

Luke 2:36-38: The prophetess Anna served God day and night in the temple with fasting and prayer. Her prayers were possibly related to her waiting for the coming Messiah.

Luke 18:11-12: The Pharisees fasted twice a week (see also Matthew 9:14).

Luke 18:9-14: Jesus condemned self-righteous boasting in fasting.

Acts 10:30: Cornelius was praying and fasting when the angel appeared to him and directed him to send for Peter. *Variations in translation related to this text are discussed in the next section.*

Acts 13:1-3: The Christians in Antioch practiced fasting. The missionary movement began during such fasting.

Acts 13:1-3: Fasting was practiced in relation to the ordination of missionaries.

Acts 14:23: Christians at Antioch fasted as part of the ordination of missionaries and elders.

Romans 14:6: Paul wrote that the believer is free to follow his conscience in the matters of observing days and eating, yet he is obligated to do all unto God and for His glory.

I Corinthians 7:5: Paul mentioned fasting and prayer as proper reasons for abstinence within the marital relationship. *Variations in translation related to this text are discussed in the next section.*

I Corinthians 9:24-27: The victorious Christian life requires self-control, including disciplining the body to make it subservient to the will of God.

II Corinthians 6:4-5: Fasting was one of the ways in which the Apostle Paul commended himself as a genuine servant of God. *Variations in translation related to this text are discussed in the next section.*

II Corinthians 11:27: The Apostle Paul fasted often in the midst of his ministry. *Variations in translation related to this text are discussed in the next section.*

Colossians 2:23: Paul declared ascetic practices and severe treatment of the body to be of no value against fleshly indulgence.

I Timothy 4:1-5: It is heretical to advocate abstaining from foods that God has created to be gratefully shared by those who believe and know the truth.

VARIATIONS IN TRANSLATION

In the above survey of biblical texts regarding fasting, we mentioned five texts that would require further discussion because of variations in translations. Before advancing further in this study, we will consider each one in detail.

MARK 9:29

Some translations (KJV/NKJV) include fasting along with prayer, while others (NASB/ESV) omit it and mention only prayer. The earliest Greek manuscripts (Alexandrian, Western, and Caesarean) do not include the additional phrase "and fasting." However, it is found in virtually all other remaining manuscripts and versions. Those conservative scholars who omit fasting believe it is a scribal insertion influenced by the early and medieval church's growing emphasis on fasting. Nevertheless, even if the phrase "and fasting" is a later insertion, it is not contrary to sound doctrine or practice. Remember that the disciples' inability to cast out the demon was only indirectly related to their lack of prayer (and/or fasting). The primary reason for their failure was their lack of spiritual authority due to their lack of faith (Matthew 10:1; Mark 9:18-19; Matthew 17:19-20). Like prayer, biblical fasting can be a means of strengthening the believer's faith and is represented throughout the Old Testament as a means of asking God for deliverance.

Acts 10:30

The KJV and NKJV describe Cornelius praying and fasting, while the NASB and ESV say that he only prayed. Again, this difference of translation is based on variants in Greek manuscripts. Some scholars argue that the reference to fasting was deleted from the account in verse 30 because it is not mentioned in the first account in verses 1-4. Others hold that the reference to fasting was a later scribal addition due to the early and medieval church's emphasis on fasting. Regardless, even if the word "fasting" is a later insertion, it is not contrary to sound doctrine or practice.

I Corinthians 7:5

Some translations (KJV/NKJV) refer to spouses devoting themselves to prayer and fasting, while others (NASB/ESV) refer only to prayer. This difference of opinion is once more based on variants in Greek manuscripts. The earliest manuscripts do not mention fasting. Therefore, many conservative scholars hold that this reference found in later manuscripts was also a scribal addition. Again, even if the word "fasting" is a later insertion, it is not contrary to sound doctrine or practice. In fact, it is not improbable that fasting might have accompanied prayer in such cases.

II Corinthians 6:5 and II Corinthians 11:27

The KJV mentions "watchings" and "fastings," while the NASB describes "sleeplessness" and "hunger." The reason for the differences is not due to variants in different manuscripts, but to differing opinions regarding the translation from Greek to English. In II Corinthians 6:5, "sleeplessness" is translated from the Greek word *agrupnía*, which can denote sleeplessness or watching. The word "hunger" is translated from the Greek word *nēsteía*, which can refer to a religious fast or a forced fast due to want, poverty, or difficult circumstances. In II Corinthians 11:27, "sleeplessness" is again translated from the Greek word *agrupnía*, but "hunger" is translated from the Greek word *limós*, which most often denotes famine, hunger, or starvation. The Apostle Paul possibly had both ideas in mind. He probably followed the example of Jesus by spending nights in prayer (Mark 1:35; Luke 6:12). There were times when he was forced to go without food due to poverty or circumstance (Philippians 4:12; I Corinthians 4:11) as well as times when he voluntarily fasted to seek the Lord.

Chapter 2: The Christian and Fasting

FASTING FOR TODAY

Some sincere Christians argue that fasting is an Old Testament practice that is not prescribed for the New Testament Christian. While it is true that the New Testament lacks any specific command regarding fasting, there is evidence in both the Old and New Testaments that supports the view that fasting is both permitted and encouraged for New Testament believers. Below, we will consider this evidence.

1. In Matthew 6:2-18, Jesus mentions three pillars or expressions of Jewish piety or devotion. Identify them in the spaces below.

    a. *When you G_____ to the poor (v.3).*

    b. *When you P_____ (v.5).*

    c. *When you F_____ (v.16).*

    > NOTES: Notice that Jesus does not say "if" you give or pray or fast but "when" you do these acts of piety. In these texts, the Lord Jesus shows that He expected His disciples to practice fasting until His return. Also note that Jesus is not commanding fasting or establishing fasting as a spiritual devotion that must be practiced by all saints at all times. Throughout the New Testament, frequent prayer (Luke 18:1; I Thessalonians 5:17) and giving (Ephesians 4:28; Hebrews 13:16; I John 3:17) are commanded for all believers. This is not the case with fasting.

2. The book of Acts reflects the history of the first-century church. How do the following texts from Acts demonstrate that fasting was practiced by the early church and is a valid practice for Christians today?

    a. *Acts 13:1-2*

    _____

    _____

    _____

    _____

    _____

b. *Acts 14:19-23*

_____

_____

_____

_____

_____

NOTES: It would be irresponsible to suggest that the only reason for these occurrences of fasting is that the believers of the early church had not come to understand their new life in Christ and were still bound by old traditions. In each case, the Apostle Paul and other leaders of the church were both present and participating in the fast.

3. Again, the New Testament does not command fasting. There are, however, positive examples of fasting throughout the Old Testament. Should these examples be regarded as authoritative directives for the believer today? What do the following texts from the New Testament teach us regarding the matter?

   a. *Romans 15:4*

_____

_____

_____

_____

_____

   b. *I Corinthians 10:11*

_____

_____

_____

_____

_____

_____

NOTES: The teaching and historical accounts of the Old Testament were written for the instruction of the New Testament church. Therefore, the Old Testament's teaching on fasting, as well as its positive and negative examples of fasting, provide a sure foundation for the practice today. Many of the most devoted saints in the Old Testament practiced fasting. This is a great testimony to the benefit and enduring importance of the practice. Those who participate in fasting are in the choice company of great saints in Scripture and in church history.

FASTING TRANSFORMED

In Matthew 9:14-17 (also in Luke 5:33-39), the disciples of John the Baptist came to Jesus and asked Him why His disciples did not fast. Many have used this question and Jesus' response to advance the teaching that the coming of Jesus has made fasting not only unnecessary but also inappropriate. However, a careful reading of the text will reveal that Jesus does not negate fasting; instead, He transforms it and fills it with new life and hope. Read Matthew 9:14-17 until you are familiar with its contents, and then complete the following exercises.

1. According to the first half of verse 15, what reason does Jesus give as to why His disciples were not fasting at that particular time?

_____

_____

_____

_____

_____

_____

NOTES: We must remember the context of Jesus' reply. His intention was not to negate the practice of fasting, but to answer why His disciples did not fast. Jesus' answer was clear and profound: at that time, the mourning and longing associated with fasting would have been inappropriate because the Bridegroom (Christ Himself) was with them. Christ incarnate was an occasion for joy and celebration.

2. According to the second half of verse 15, when would it be appropriate for Christ's disciples to fast? Explain your answer.

_____

_____

_____

_____

_____

_____

_____

NOTES: It would be entirely appropriate for Christ's disciples to fast: (1) when the Bridegroom was violently taken away from them and crucified, and (2) throughout the entire age of the church—a time that would be marked by suffering, need, and spiritual warfare; a time in which Christ's disciples would need to draw upon His provision through prayer and fasting; a time in which they would long for the fullness of Christ's presence and watch for His return.

3. Jesus affirms the continuation of fasting among His disciples in the Sermon on the Mount (Matthew 6:16-18), and He does not negate its usefulness here in Matthew 9. However, in verses 16-17, He does use two picturesque illustrations to communicate that there would be important differences between the kind of fasting associated with the Pharisees and John's disciples and that of the church. What illustrations does Jesus use?

a. *U_____ C_____ on old garments.* A new, unshrunk cloth cannot be used to patch an old shrunken garment: when the new cloth shrinks, it will tear the old garment, leaving it in even worse condition.

b. *N_____ W_____ into old wineskins.* New wine cannot be stored in old, dried wineskins: the old and brittle wineskins will break open when the new wine ferments and expands, and all will be lost.

NOTES: Jesus likens the fasting of both the Pharisees and John's disciples to an old garment and an old wineskin. In the case of the Pharisees, fasting had become an empty tradition, an external ritual, and a scheduled discipline (see Luke 18:11-12). In the case of John's disciples, fasting was marked by mourning, affliction, and a longing for deliverance through the Messiah. In light of these two facts, it is obvious how Christian fasting should differ not only from the empty customs of the Pharisees but also from the fasting of the sincere disciples of John. Unlike the Pharisees, the fasting that Jesus prescribed was born out of a heartfelt passion and longing for God. This fasting went far beyond the Pharisaical notion of a traditional ritual to be observed on certain days, a mandatory practice, or a religious exercise. Unlike John's disciples, Christ's disciples would not fast as those who were awaiting redemption, but as those who had already experienced it! There would still be suffering, mourning, and longing throughout the long ages of the church; but Christ's disciples and their fasting would be infused with the reality of Christ's presence, the assurance of His salvation, and the great expectation that "everyone who asks receives, and he who seeks finds, and to him who knocks it will be opened" (Matthew 7:8). Christ's coming has changed absolutely everything! His finished work on Calvary, the hope and power of His resurrection, and His sending of the Spirit have made all things new, even fasting. Our new life in Christ is the fulfillment of the promise of Old Testament prophesy—foreshadowed in Old Testament rituals and longed for by Old Testament saints. Although we still await the restoration of all things at the second coming of Jesus, the Kingdom of Heaven has come and infused our lives with joy, fulfillment, and great expectation. We do not fast in response to a prescribed or legalistic ritual; we fast in response to a heartfelt passion for God. We do not fast because we are barren; we fast because we have tasted and seen that the Lord is good—this fullness has made us desire Him even more! We do not fast because the kingdom has not come; we fast because it **has** come and because we long for its extension into every corner of our lives and every corner of the earth.

4. Based on the texts that we have studied and the truths that we have considered, write a brief explanation regarding the validity of fasting in the church and the distinctive characteristics of Christian fasting.

   a. *Is fasting a valid spiritual discipline for the Christian today? Write your thoughts.*

   _____

   _____

   _____

   _____

   _____

   _____

   _____

b. *What are some of the important distinctives of Christian fasting? How does Christian fasting contrast with that of the Pharisees and the followers of John the Baptist?*

_____

_____

_____

_____

_____

_____

_____

_____

_____

Chapter 3: Fasting as a Response of the Heart

This brief chapter is arguably the most important in this entire study because it seeks to explain the very heart of fasting—answering the question, "Why do we fast?" The fundamental truth that we will seek to convey is that **fasting is a result of a passion, desire, or need that drives out all others—including, at times, the necessity and delight of food and other temporal pleasures.**

A RESPONSE OF THE HEART

Fasting is the response of a heart that is so consumed with a certain desire or need that it foregoes temporal pleasures and even the necessities of life in order to seek the fulfillment of that desire. However, it is important to note that the passion or desire that consumes and drives a person to fast may be godly or carnal. Moses fasted for Israel's pardon because of his love for his people and his zeal for God's glory (Exodus 34:27-28). David was moved by love and pity to fast for his dying son (II Samuel 12:15-23). Anna fasted in the temple out of devotion to God and a longing for the Messiah (Luke 2:36-38). In contrast, Saul's fear and self-pity drove out his desire for food (I Samuel 28:20). Similarly, Ahab was so consumed by his illicit desire for Naboth's vineyard that he would not eat (I Kings 21:4). Finally, the Pharisees' desire for the glory of men drove them to fast twice a week (Matthew 6:16; Luke 18:11-12).

In the book of Psalms, there are two texts that will help us understand the nature of fasting and its motives. Although they do not directly relate to fasting, they demonstrate a key principle in fasting. The first text comes from Psalm 102:4, where the psalmist cries out, "My heart has been smitten like grass and has withered away, indeed, *I forget to eat my bread*" (emphasis added). Here we see that the psalmist's affliction and his desire to be free from it drove out mere temporal concerns. Food was no longer his delight; it did not even enter into his mind. The second text comes from Psalm 107:17-18, where we see the people of God suffering to such a degree that "their *soul abhorred* all kinds of food" (emphasis added). Their affliction was so great and their desire to be free from it was so intense that food was not just undesirable—it was abhorrent. Their attitude toward food could be summarized by the question, "How can we even think of eating at a time like this?"

In both of the above texts, food was forgotten, even abhorred, because of affliction and the desire to be free from it. This cause-and-effect relationship is the foundation of fasting and can be applied to all sorts of needs and desires. We fast whenever a certain desire or need that God alone can supply drives out temporal pleasures and drives us to seek God.

- We may be so afflicted and so desirous of deliverance that we forget our food and continue in prayer to God.

- We may set aside food and temporal joys because God exposes a certain sin in our lives, causing us to sense the urgent need for reconciliation, restoration, and power to gain mastery over it.

- We may forget our food because of our zeal for God's name and because of the godless who reproach it.

- We may be so overwhelmed with concern for the purity of the church or the conversion of the nations that we set aside food for the purpose of intercession.

- We may forget every thought of food and desire for temporal joy because of our satisfaction in God's presence and the joy of continued communion with Him.

In summary, the Christian may fast for all sorts of reasons. However, all true fasting shares one thing in common: we fast when a need, sorrow, or godly desire becomes so strong and all-consuming that we literally "forget our bread" in order to seek God in prayer. The following illustrations may be helpful.

Suppose there is a man who has planned and labored for several years to travel abroad. Yet at the moment of his departure, his young son falls gravely ill. At that moment, the man does not regret the loss of a long-anticipated vacation; the very thought of it has been driven from his mind. It has been pushed out by a far greater love and a far greater need. In a similar fashion, the Christian may forgo food and other temporal pleasures because of an overwhelming desire for the healing of a fellow Christian, the evangelization of an unreached people group, or the welfare of an entire nation. He does not regret the loss of food, fellowship, or temporal delights; they have been driven out of his heart and mind by a greater desire.

Consider a son who has become aware that his less-than-virtuous actions have gravely dishonored his father. He fears the harm he may have done to his father's name. He is sick with self-reproach. He earnestly desires to make amends, to rectify his wrong, and to find his father and gain his pardon. He can no longer think of temporal joys, the fellowship of close friends, or the delights of entertainment and food. He must find his father, he must have a hearing, and he must be reconciled. Similarly, a Christian may become aware that his sin has gravely dishonored God and may be filled with godly sorrow, indignation, fear, longing, and a desire for pardon. He cannot find peace or joy in any temporal pleasure until he finds God in prayer and is assured of pardon.

Imagine a wife whose husband is called to duty as a soldier in a distant land. At times, she so longs for him that she forgets or forgoes the daily routine of eating. Her desire for her husband's companionship drives out her desire for even her most basic needs and common pleasures. She reads over his letters, gazes upon photographs, and waits for every call. In those special times when her husband does call, the wife spends the entire day and evening on the phone with him. The hours pass by unnoticed. Breakfast, lunch, and dinner are missed without the slightest grief. Her joy is so great that she retires to bed but can hardly sleep for thoughts of him. Likewise, the Christian may forgo food and temporal pleasures because of an overwhelming desire to seek God's presence in prayer, commune with Him, and read His Word. Furthermore, there will be those special times in prayer when God manifests His presence in a special visitation and the Christian is engulfed in Him. All else is forgotten! Morning, afternoon, and evening pass as though they were only moments; and the Christian retires to bed with joy unspeakable and full of glory!

A LITMUS TEST OF THE HEART

Before we conclude this chapter, an important point must be made. As we have already stated and will state again, fasting is not commanded in the Scriptures. Furthermore, fasting should not be required or declared compulsory, and it should not be exalted as a mark of maturity or spirituality. Nevertheless, fasting may function as something of a litmus test for the kind of passions that govern us or control our lives. As genuine fasting reveals a passion for God and a dependence upon His power as well as a concern for others, the neglect of fasting may be an indicator of apathy toward God and an excessive delight in or dependence upon self and the temporal pleasures of this world.

Are we so satisfied with this world and its temporal pleasures that we never long for God or ache for a greater measure of His presence? Are we so satisfied with our spiritual status quo that we have no zeal for greater conformity to the will of God and the image of Christ? Are we so apathetic to the needs and sufferings of others that we are never driven to passionate intercession for them? In summary, are we not in danger when our passion for God's glory, our desire for greater sanctification, and our concern for the needs of others rarely overpower our desires for food and temporal entertainments? As we will learn in this study, fasting is not represented in the Scriptures as a necessarily frequent practice or a scheduled ritual. However, if it is entirely absent from our lives, it may be an indication of either ignorance or apathy.

Chapter 4: Fasting Upward

Part One: Seeking and Worshiping God

Having affirmed that fasting is a valid practice for the Christian and the church collectively, we will now consider several of the Scriptural reasons or motives for fasting from three different perspectives—**upward**, **inward**, and **outward**. We will begin with fasting upward, which is fasting for the purposes of seeking God, ministering to God, and discerning God's will. Before we delve in, note that although we will be considering some of the major reasons or motivations for fasting, this study is not at all exhaustive. There are countless reasons for the believer and the church to fast that time and space will not allow us to mention.

SEEKING GOD

According to the Bible, every believer is complete in Christ (Colossians 2:10), indwelt by the Holy Spirit (Romans 8:9), and granted a filial relationship with the Father (Romans 8:14-16; Galatians 4:6-7). However, these biblical realities should not make us complacent. Instead, we should take full advantage of our new position in Christ and strive to avail ourselves of all the precious and magnificent promises that have been laid before us in the Scriptures—promises of greater knowledge of God; greater intimacy with Him; and greater manifestations of His presence, life, and power. The taste of God we received at conversion should fill us with the desire for more, and each new manifestation of His grace should drive us to seek the impossible—to exhaust every promise and privilege that He has granted us. At times, this desire may be so overwhelming that we turn away from temporal pleasures to seek greater fullness and satisfaction in God.

1. The following are some of the most beautiful and powerful texts in the Scriptures regarding a longing or hunger for God. Consider each text, and write your thoughts. How should this kind of longing be reflected in our lives?

   a. *Psalm 27:4*

   _____

   _____

   _____

   _____

   _____

_____
_____
_____

b. *Psalm 42:1-2*

_____
_____
_____
_____
_____
_____
_____

c. *Psalm 63:1*

_____
_____
_____
_____
_____
_____
_____

2. In Psalm 4:6-7, David declares that God has put more gladness in his heart than when the grain and new wine abounded. Then in Psalm 34:8, David admonishes us to "taste and see that the Lord is good." How do these texts prove that God is more satisfying than food? How do they encourage us to set aside temporal pleasures for a time, that we might know God and experience greater intimacy with Him?

_____

_____

_____

_____

_____

_____

_____

_____

_____

WORSHIPING GOD

Worship is the great end of all our longing and seeking after God. We were created and redeemed to worship Him. In fact, it is no exaggeration to say that worship is the Christian's greatest occupation. The Scriptures teach that we are to worship God by offering our lives to Him as a living sacrifice (Romans 12:1-2) and by doing all things for His glory (I Corinthians 10:31). However, the Scriptures also call us to the great privilege of devoting ourselves to specific times of worship and ministering unto the Lord. In these times, fasting can be a great blessing and benefit.

1. In Luke 2:36-37, we read about the prophetess Anna of the tribe of Asher. She was extremely devoted to God and was awaiting the coming of the Messiah. According to verse 37, how did Anna demonstrate her devotion to the Lord? How did she serve the Lord? How might the Christian do the same?

_____

_____

_____

_____

_____

_____

_____

_____

NOTES: The word "serving" comes from the Greek word *latreúō*, which denotes both service and worship (Matthew 4:10; Philippians 3:3; Hebrews 10:2). It is used in the final chapter of the Scriptures to describe our service to God in the new heaven and the new earth (Revelation 22:3). We rarely think that serving the Lord through worship includes fasting and praying; these acts of service, however, are some of the most pleasing to Him. This reminds us of how much we can exhibit the busyness of Martha by being distracted by so many things. We could learn a great deal from Mary, who chose the "good part" and sat quietly at the feet of Jesus (Luke 10:39-42).

2. Unlike Anna, we may not be called to dedicate ourselves entirely to fasting and prayer. There are many other things to be accomplished, such as the Great Commission and the edification of the church! However, even the most active believers and ministers must learn to turn aside from their activity and dedicate themselves to ministering unto the Lord. According to Acts 13:1-2, what were the Apostle Paul, several teachers and prophets, and possibly the entire church in Antioch doing immediately prior to the birth of one of the greatest missionary movements the world has ever known?

   a. M_____ *to the Lord and* F_____. The word "ministering" comes from the Greek word *leitourgéō* and is used with reference to the ministry of the Levitical priests in the tabernacle or temple (Exodus 28:43; 29:30; Luke 1:23; Hebrews 10:11). The Christian is now part of a royal priesthood (I Peter 2:9) and is called to offer a sacrifice of praise unto God (Hebrews 13:15). It is a great privilege and extremely beneficial for the believer to devote periods of time to worshiping and ministering to the Lord. Fasting can be an excellent accompaniment to these holy and royal activities.

3. What have you learned from this section about ministering to the Lord with prayer and fasting? How might you apply what you have learned to your own life?

   _____

   _____

Chapter 5: Fasting Upward

Part Two: Discerning God's Will

The entirety of the Christian's life must be founded upon and directed by the will of God. All that we think and speak and do must be conformed to His design. For this reason, our discerning of God's will is absolutely essential. In the following Scriptures from the New Testament, we will learn that the seeking of God's will was at times accompanied by fasting and that God's will was revealed when believers were fasting specifically for that purpose. This does not mean that we must fast before making every decision regarding the will of God. The greatest portion of everything we need to know about God's will is revealed to us in the Scriptures (Psalm 119:9, 105). The Scriptures also admonish us to seek godly counsel whenever important decisions are to be made (Proverbs 11:14; 12:15; 13:10). However, at times, when the way is unclear and absolute certainty is required, it is appropriate to seek the Lord through worship, prayer, and fasting.

1. In Daniel 9:2, we read that Daniel was seeking to understand the will of God through Jeremiah's prophecies regarding the desolation of Jerusalem and the return of the exiles. According to verse 3, how did Daniel seek an answer to his questions? According to verses 21-23, how did God respond? What can we learn from these texts about fasting and the will of God?

    _____

    _____

    _____

    _____

    _____

    _____

    _____

NOTES: The will of God is revealed to us through the Scriptures; therefore, we are not dependent upon dreams, visions, or angelic visitations. However, the truths of Scripture are spiritually discerned and require the illumination of the Holy Spirit (I Corinthians 2:12-16). Therefore, we should read the Scriptures in prayerful dependence upon God to teach us. As we see from the example of Daniel, fasting can play a part in seeking and discerning the will of God.

2. The appointment of elders (pastors) in a church is one of the most important decisions that a congregation will ever have to make. For this reason, it is extremely important that the church clearly discern the Lord's will in the matter. What was involved in the selecting and commissioning of elders in Acts 14:23?

   a. *The believers P_____ with F_____.* Even though the selection and commission process involved two of the most respected leaders in the early church (the Apostle Paul and Barnabas), the believers still prayed and fasted. We must not be apathetic about the will of God or merely presume that He will lead us regardless of what we do. Instead, we should be diligent to employ the means given to us to correctly discern His will and make the right choices. This truth is powerfully reflected in the life of our Lord Jesus Christ, who spent the entire night in prayer before selecting and commissioning the twelve apostles (Luke 6:12-13). It is also important to note that these examples are not grounds for **requiring** fasting before the selection of elders; they only demonstrate that it is **appropriate** to fast when determined necessary. The Apostle Paul does not mention fasting in the two most important passages on eldership (I Timothy 3:1-7; Titus 1:5-9).

3. In Acts 13:1-3, we witness a truly extraordinary event—the birth of one of the greatest missionary movements the world has ever known. At this time, God, through the Holy Spirit, directed the church in Antioch to set apart Barnabas and Saul (the Apostle Paul) for the evangelization of the Gentiles. According to verse 2, in what context did God reveal His will to the church? In what activities were the believers occupied? What can we learn from this?

   _____

   _____

   _____

   _____

   _____

   _____

NOTES: As the believers in Antioch were devoting themselves to worship and fasting, the Lord revealed to them His will regarding the evangelization of the Gentiles and the men who should lead the endeavor—Barnabas and Saul (the Apostle Paul). The truth conveyed is this: the more we set aside time to draw near to God in worship and prayer and even fasting, the more discerning we will be with regard to His will and the more useful we will be with regard to His purposes.

4. God graciously and clearly reveals His will to us through the Scriptures. The Scriptures also admonish us to seek counsel from godly, mature Christians who can help us discern the will of God. However, there are also times when major decisions must be made and the way is unclear. During these times we may seek the will of God through prayer and fasting. In the space below, list some major decisions about which you should seek the Lord with fasting.

_____

_____

_____

_____

_____

_____

NOTES: As we seek the Lord in prayer, the Holy Spirit may impress His will upon our hearts and minds. However, we must proceed with caution. Not all impressions are from God, and our hearts and minds are easily deceived. The only infallible standard regarding God's will is Scripture. Therefore, we must compare all thoughts, impressions, and human counsel to the inerrant words of Scripture. We must reject anything that contradicts *what is written!*

Chapter 6: Fasting Inward

Part One: Identifying Sin

In the previous chapters, we considered three very important reasons that believers might fast: to seek God, to worship God, and to discern God's will. In these next chapters, we will consider **fasting inward**—fasting for the purposes of self-examination, repentance, and victory over sin.

TESTING AND SELF-EXAMINATION

Fasting provides a powerful context for testing and self-examination. When we remove the pleasures and comforts of food, we have the opportunity to see our "true selves" more clearly. This is one of the most beneficial aspects of fasting, yet it is often overlooked by the majority of believers.

It is far easier for us to demonstrate godliness and mask the hidden flaws in our character when our basic needs are being met and our circumstances are pleasant. A melancholy man may exhibit joy when all is going his way; a greedy man may practice generosity during times of his own prosperity; and an impatient man may demonstrate longsuffering toward others if his own circumstances are agreeable to him. However, when circumstances take a turn for the worse, their actions follow suit, and their true characters are often revealed.

To further illustrate this truth, we only need to think about how we make excuses for our irritated and impatient behavior. We often say that we are not "acting like ourselves" because of a certain physical illness or difficult circumstance. However, the very opposite is true! The illness or difficult circumstance reveals the true self that had been masked by more acceptable circumstances. This shows that the affliction did not make us irritable or impatient but revealed the irritability and impatience that were lying hidden. Thus, we discover that we are often like children who appear serene and well-behaved until their desires are taken from them—then they throw a tantrum, and their true characters are revealed.

Although we should not purposely seek out adverse circumstances or trials in order to test our faith and character, they are an important part of God's sanctifying work in our lives and should be welcomed (Romans 5:3; James 1:2). Biblical fasting serves a similar purpose as a trial in that it not only removes a basic need but also takes from us something that for many has wrongly become a primary source of joy and comfort—food and the companionship associated with it! Our true character is exposed through fasting by removing the external props of temporal pleasures, and we are given the opportunity to deal with our hidden sin through repentance and greater dependence on Christ.

1. Matthew 4:1-11 records the temptation of Jesus in the wilderness. In verses 1-3, we discover three truths that can be applied to the believer and fasting.

   a. *Jesus was L_____ by the S_____ into the W_____ (v.1).*
      The Gospel of Mark tells us that the Spirit literally "impelled" or "cast out" Jesus into the

wilderness. In fact, Mark uses the same Greek word (**ekbállō**) that is used to describe the "casting out" of demons. The idea expressed is that it was the will of God that Christ be tested in the wilderness. In a similar way, it is the will of God that believers pass through times of testing in order that their true character might be revealed and addressed through repentance and faith (I Peter 1:6-7).

b. *Jesus F_____ and became H_____ (v.2).* The true character of Christ was revealed while He was in the worst of circumstances, unaided by even the most basic pleasantries of life such as food and companionship. The wilderness and the fasting acted as a crucible to reveal Christ's true mettle (Hebrews 4:15). The application to fasting is apparent. Unaided by the pleasantries of food and the companionship that often accompanies eating, our true characters are more clearly revealed and sin is more clearly exposed. This affords us the opportunity to deal with these hidden sins by means of repentance and faith.

c. *The T_____ came to Him (v.3).* As in the wilderness temptation of Christ, the devil may draw near to us when we fast in order to accuse, condemn, and tempt us. However, his evil can turn out for our good if we resist him, draw near to God, cleanse our hands, and purify our hearts (James 4:7-8). Every sin exposed should lead us to confession. Every temptation should create in us a greater dependence upon God.

2. Based on the truths we have gleaned from Matthew 4:1-3, how might fasting aid us in obeying the admonition from Lamentations 3:40, "Let us examine and probe our ways, and let us return to the Lord"?

_____

_____

_____

_____

_____

_____

_____

_____

_____

_____

REPENTANCE

Throughout the Old Testament, fasting is most often identified with brokenness over sin, repentance, and confession. However, it is important to understand that fasting is not required to obtain forgiveness from God. We obtain forgiveness and restoration through genuine repentance and faith in Christ. Fasting is simply the response of the believer who has realized something of the heinous nature of his sin and is so broken over his offense, so fearful of the devastating consequence of sin, and so desirous to set things right that all temporal pleasures are forgotten in order to seek God's fellowship and aid.

1. In II Corinthians 7:11, we are given a powerful picture of genuine or biblical repentance. Identify each characteristic according to the text.

    a. E_____. This is from the Greek word **spoudê**, which denotes diligence and eagerness or an earnest and eager desire to do the right thing.

    b. G_____ S_____. The word "godly" is translated from the Greek phrase **katá theón** or "toward God." Godly sorrow is God-ward. The truly repentant are not merely sorrowful because of the weight of their guilt or the effect their sin might have upon them; they are sorrowful primarily because they have offended God.

    c. V_____. This is from the Greek word **apología**, which refers to a verbal defense or clearing of one's name. The truly repentant believer desires to do the right thing to prove his renewed commitment to God's will and to vindicate himself. He wants to bear fruit in keeping with repentance (Matthew 3:8).

    d. I_____. This is from the Greek word **aganáktēsis**, which denotes indignation, irritation, and vexation. There is a very real sense in which the truly repentant believer will be angry with himself because of the sin he has committed (Ephesians 4:26-27).

    e. F_____. This word refers to the fear of God, the fear of remaining outside of His will, and the fear of the devastating consequences of sin. It proves that the repentant believer has a real understanding of the heinousness and dangerous consequences of sin.

    f. L_____. This is from the Greek word **epipóthēsis**, which denotes an earnest, passionate, and even vehement desire or longing. The truly repentant believer has a longing for holiness, restoration, and renewed communion with God and other believers.

    g. Z_____. This term is from the Greek word **zêlos**, which denotes fervor or intense devotion. It is the opposite of apathy or indifference.

    h. A_____ of wrong. This is from the Greek word **ekdíkēsis**, which denotes the rendering of justice—even vengeance. This is not directed toward a person but refers to the believer's commitment to see justice done and wrongs rectified.

2. As we have already stated, fasting is often associated with repentance throughout the Old Testament. Below are several examples of both individual and corporate repentance accompanied by fasting. They illustrate many of the truths that we discovered in II Corinthians 7:11. Summarize each text in your own words. What can we learn about repentance and fasting from these texts?

a. *Nehemiah 1:3-10*

_____

_____

_____

_____

_____

_____

_____

NOTES: These are the key elements in Nehemiah's fasting: mourning and weeping over the distress and reproach of God's people (vv.3-4), prayer (v.4), confession of sin (vv.6-7), and petition for deliverance based upon God's character (v.5) and His promises (vv.8-10).

b. *Nehemiah 9:1-3*

_____

_____

_____

_____

_____

_____

NOTES: These are the key elements in Israel's fasting: humility and mourning (v.1), separation from the ungodly (v.2), confession of sin and worship (vv.2-3), and reading from God's Law (v.3). Notice the direct relationship between the Law or Word of

God, the exposing of sin in the believer's life, and the confession of sin. All brokenness, confession, and fasting must be based upon the revelation of God's will through
His Word.

c. *Daniel 9:3-5, 17-19*

_____

_____

_____

_____

_____

_____

NOTES: These are the key elements in Daniel's fasting: prayer and supplication for forgiveness and restoration (vv.3, 17-19), humility and mourning denoted by the sackcloth
and ashes (v.3), confession of the faithfulness of God (v.4), and confession of the sin
of God's people (v.5). Notice that the basis of Daniel's petition for Israel's pardon was
neither Israel's merit, nor the merit of Daniel's fasting, but the character of God (v.18).

d. *Joel 2:12-13*

_____

_____

_____

_____

_____

_____

NOTES: These are the key elements in the fasting revealed through the prophet Joel: a returning to God that indicates a turning from sin (v.12), genuine brokenness manifested in weeping and mourning (vv.12-13), and hope in the character and promises of God (v.13). Notice that fasting must never be reduced to an external ritual (*i.e.* an outward appearance of affliction, like the rending of garments). True fasting is the result of an internal reality (*i.e.* true sorrow for sin or a rending of the heart).

e. *Jonah 3:4-10*

_____

_____

_____

_____

_____

_____

_____

NOTES: These are the key elements in Nineveh's fasting: belief in the Word of God (v.4); humility from the greatest to the least, even the king (v.5-6); mourning, denoted by sackcloth and ashes (vv.6-8); earnest prayer (v.8); renouncing and turning from sin (v.8); and hope in the mercies of God (vv.9-10).

3. Acts 9 records the conversion of Saul of Tarsus, the greatest persecutor of the early church. After his encounter with the glorified Jesus on the road to Damascus, Saul is left blinded and must be led by hand into the city. According to verse 9, what was Saul's initial reaction to his encounter and conversion? What can be learned from this event about repentance and fasting?

_____

_____

_____

_____

_____

_____

_____

NOTES: After the encounter with the risen Jesus, Paul's life is left in shambles; his entire reality disintegrates. He comes to understand that he has been wrong about everything. Although physically blinded, he sees the light for the first time in his life. Paul's dramatic conversion and his immediate response are not to be held up as a pattern for every believer. Nevertheless, there are some things that we can learn from his experience. First, our transgression is a serious matter that should not be taken lightly. When God reveals our sin to us, we should respond with earnest contemplation. Second, any revelation of the truth is a serious matter whereby we become stewards of that truth. We should never be careless with truth. We should guard it in our hearts, ponder its meaning, and determine an appropriate response. Third, there are occasions of solemnity and gravity that require separation from the daily routine so that we might consider what the Lord has done and what He desires to do in our lives. Fasting can be an important part of this activity, especially in light of the frivolity and busyness of our age!

4. In all the Scriptures, there is one example of repentance with fasting that stands out above the others as a demonstration of God's grace and willingness to forgive. The Scriptures tell us that King Ahab did evil in the sight of the Lord more than all who were before him (I Kings 16:30) and that he did more to provoke the Lord God of Israel than all the kings of Israel who were before him (I Kings 16:33). As a response to Ahab's evil, God sent the prophet Elijah to pronounce a terrifying declaration of divine judgment upon him. According to I Kings 21:27-29, what was Ahab's response? What then was God's response to Ahab? What does this teach us about the character of God? How may these truths be applied to the believer?

_____

_____

_____

_____

_____

_____

_____

_____

NOTES: The Lord is compassionate, gracious, slow to anger, forgiving, and abounding in lovingkindness and truth (Exodus 34:6-7). If God was so willing to forgive the wicked King Ahab, will He not also be disposed to forgive His children? In Romans 8:31-35, the Apostle Paul asks: "What then shall we say to these things? If God is for us, who is against us? He who did not spare His own Son, but delivered Him over for us all, how will He not also with Him freely give us all things? Who will bring a charge against God's elect? God is the one who justifies; who is the one who condemns? Christ Jesus is He who died, yes, rather who was raised, who is at the right hand of God, who also intercedes for us. Who will separate us from the love of Christ?"

Chapter 7: Fasting Inward
Part Two: Battling Sin

Repentance is not an end in itself, but our desire should be to grow in grace and gain mastery over self and victory over sin. The most frequently mentioned means of grace for growth in sanctification are the Word of God (study, meditation, and memorization) and prayer, yet fasting can also be a useful means of gaining greater victory over sin and greater mastery over the desires of the flesh.

VICTORY OVER SIN

The Christian is freed from the condemnation of sin (Romans 8:1) and is no longer enslaved to sin (Romans 6:6). Nevertheless, the Christian is not free from the battle against sin (Galatians 5:17). The flesh, the world, and the devil are all in league to defeat the Christian and destroy his testimony. For this reason, we should do everything within our means to stand firm. Study and application of God's Word and devotion to prayer are not the only means of grace at our disposal. Throughout the history of the church, the practice of fasting has also been a means to strengthen the believer in his battle against sin.

In any biblical study, we must let the Scriptures speak for themselves, drawing our doctrine from the Word rather than taking it out of context to form our own doctrine. There are no texts in Scripture that speak directly about fasting as a means of gaining victory over sin or overcoming a certain sin that might be encumbering or entangling us (Hebrews 12:1). However, fasting is mentioned with prayer as a spiritual discipline to aid in the advancement of the kingdom and our personal progress in godliness (Matthew 6:5, 16). Furthermore, fasting is often mentioned alongside prayer in times of great need, when God's favor and power are an absolute necessity—in times of confession; repentance; and pleas for deliverance from enemies, illnesses, and afflictions. For this reason, there is a biblical foundation for including fasting as a means of seeking victory over sin. This is especially true when dealing with sins that seem to have gained a foothold in our lives and continue to prevail against us.

MASTERY OVER SELF

In the Beatitudes, Jesus taught that the pure in heart would be blessed (Matthew 5:8). This literally refers to the person who has no competing loyalties in his heart. Later in the Sermon on the Mount, Jesus warned His disciples that they could not serve more than one master, because they would hate the one and love the other or be devoted to one and despise the other (Matthew 6:24). For this reason, the Christian must be diligent to examine his heart and do all within his means to assure that he is unmastered by both sin and even the good things that the Lord may give him to enjoy. It is not uncommon for the believer to come to the point of cherishing the gift more than the Giver. Fasting can be a means of revealing other loves and other masters in our lives so that we might deal with them through repentance and faith.

UNDERSTANDING THE DISCIPLINE OF FASTING

This aspect of fasting is of special importance for Christians living in developed countries, where there is a certain degree of prosperity and ease of life. Prosperity and freedom from great suffering are not evil in themselves. They do, however, subject the believer to the temptation of drawing purpose, comfort, joy, and satisfaction from material things, pleasant circumstances, and temporal joys rather than from God. This can lead to hidden idolatry in the heart of the believer. Removing ourselves from temporal blessing and devoting ourselves to prayer and fasting can reveal these hidden idols and help us gain mastery over them.

1. In I Corinthians 6:12, the Apostle Paul corrects the erroneous teaching that the Christian is free to participate in anything he or she desires. According to the apostle, our freedom is restricted to that which is profitable for our further growth in godliness. He then makes a powerful statement that applies not only to unbiblical desires but also to desires for things that are approved by the Scriptures.

    a. *I will not be M_____ by A_____*. The word "mastered" comes from the Greek word **exousiázō**, which means, "to have power or authority over another" or "to be a master of another." Jesus claimed to have all authority (noun form of the same verb) over heaven and earth. Paul determined to be controlled by Christ and His revealed will, taking every thought captive to the obedience of Christ (II Corinthians 10:5). He would not be mastered by the lusts that the Scriptures prohibited or by the liberties that the Scriptures allowed. Christ would be the Master of his heart, the focus of his life, and the source of his satisfaction.

2. In I Corinthians 9:24-27, the Apostle Paul compares the Christian life to athletic games; he makes several important statements demonstrating that discipline in the Christian life is to be taken seriously. What are these statements? What do they mean for the Christian?

    a. *There is an imperishable P_____ to win (vv.24-25)*. A prize or wreath was awarded to the victor in an athletic competition. This wreath was perishable or subject to corruption [Greek: **phthartós**]. In contrast, the Christian's reward is incorruptible and eternal [Greek: **áphthartos**]. If it is reasonable for an athlete to train his entire life for a fleeting moment of glory and a wreath that quickly perishes, how much more should the Christian train or discipline himself to win eternal glory and a reward that is incorruptible!

    b. *We must R_____ in such a way that we may W_____ (v.24)*. The competitive and combative nature of the Christian life is a reality. A person may win eternal reward or suffer eternal loss. The competition, however, is not between Christians. It is between the Christian and that which would oppose him, including his physical body and fallen flesh. The Christian life is like an athletic competition that promises great reward for those who overcome with holy ambition, purpose, strategy, and self-control (Revelation 21:7). However, there is no consolation prize for merely participating.

    c. *We must learn to E_____ S_____ in all things (v.25)*. The word "exercise" comes from the Greek word **agōnízomai**, which means, "to strive zealously and strenuously to obtain something." The word was used with regard to competing in an athletic contest or fighting against adversaries. The word "self-control" comes from the Greek word **egkrateúomai**, which denotes the kind of self-control or self-government that is exhibited by an athlete who is preparing for a contest. He will purpose to abstain from any food or activity that might hinder his performance.

d. *We must R_____ as not without A_____ (v.26).* The great goal of Paul's life was to be pleasing to the Lord (II Corinthians 5:9). Thus, he ordered his entire life to achieve this goal. He did not live haphazardly, but intentionally, just as an Olympian orders every aspect of his life to gain the prize. Paul was not running wildly, but with a specific direction: to win the heavenly reward! He had an eye on the finish line (Philippians 3:13-14)!

e. *We must B_____ not as B_____ the air (v.26).* Again, we see purpose, intentionality, and strategy. Paul fought to win and did nothing haphazardly. He did not swing to miss but to hit exactly where he was aiming. Like a good athlete, he identified the weaknesses in his life and sought to remedy them so that he might achieve his goal.

f. *We must D_____ our B_____ (v.27).* The word "discipline" comes from the Greek word **hupōpiázō**, which means, "to beat black and blue" or "to strike with such intensity as to cause bruises." The boxer will put himself through rigorous training to toughen and harden his body so that it might endure in the midst of a fight. Likewise, Paul did not pamper his body or give in to its cry for leniency. He sought to live in the power of the Spirit and not give in to the weaknesses of his physical body or the sinful desires of his flesh.

g. *We must make our body our S_____ (v.27).* The phrase is translated from the Greek word **doulagōgéō**, which means, "to lead away into slavery." This word is used with regard to a victor who leads his vanquished foe away as a slave. Paul's physical needs and temporal desires did not control his life; rather, in the power of the Holy Spirit and according to the will of God, he controlled them. He made them subservient to the will of God and the purpose of the gospel. We must remember that the body is not evil; however, it is subject to weakness and the temptation of amenities such as ease, comfort, safety, and pleasure. Amid the demands of discipline, it is always crying out for leniency.

h. *Having considered these statements, write your thoughts. What do these truths mean for the believer?*

_____

_____

_____

_____

_____

> **NOTES:** In I Corinthians 9:26-27, the Apostle Paul writes that he disciplined his body (literally, "beat it black and blue"). However, in Colossians 2:23, he warns that severe treatment of the body (*i.e.* subjecting it to some form of monastic torture) is of no value against fleshly indulgence, nor will it make the believer more holy. There is no contradiction. In I Corinthians 9, Paul is admonishing us to discipline our bodies to make them subservient to the great purpose of living for and serving Christ. The athlete subjects his body to hard discipline and training; this is not because he hates his body or seeks to destroy it, but because he desires to make it stronger and more prepared to win the race. In the heat of the race or fight, the physical body desires to relent, to give way, to yield. However, through hard training and discipline, it must be taught to ignore the pain and endure to a victorious end.

3. In Philippians 3:18-19, the Apostle Paul describes the false prophets and teachers who were literally "enemies of the cross of Christ." Not only was their teaching false, but their mindset and lifestyle were in complete contradiction to the example in I Corinthians 9:24-27. In Philippians 3:19, Paul exposes three vices or manifestations of the flesh that marked these men. Identify each in the spaces below.

   a. *Their G_____ was their A_____.* The word "appetite" is translated from the Greek work *koilía*, which literally means, "belly" or "stomach." The reference is not limited to food but encompasses all human desires. Although both our appetite and food are gifts from God, they can become idols in our lives. Food must be a major part of our lives if we are to be healthy. However, our desire for food (and all other temporal pleasures) can become inordinate or excessive. It can become our chief desire, support, and comfort instead of God. It can also become a false prop to virtue and a mask that underlies sin. The discipline of fasting can reveal if this is the case with us and can help us to gain mastery over it.

   b. *Their G_____ was in their S_____.* The context suggests that these false teachers were unconverted men who gloried in (*i.e.* boasted in, reveled in) the shameful deeds of the flesh (Galatians 5:19-21). It is a shameful thing to desire anything, even gifts from God, above God. Fasting can reveal our true desires and uncover the source from which we seek satisfaction and comfort, be it God or temporal pleasures. It can also help us to realign our desires to what is truly worthy—God and His kingdom.

   c. *They S_____ their M_____ on E_____ things.* Paul exhorts believers in Colossians 3:1-2, "Therefore if you have been raised up with Christ, keep seeking the things above, where Christ is, seated at the right hand of God. Set your mind on the things above, not on the things that are on earth." Even believers can lose their focus and stray in their hearts. Fasting can reveal to us the focus of our minds and the true passion of our hearts. It can help us to turn our desires back to God.

Chapter 8: Fasting Inward

Part Three: Evaluating Self

INWARD EVALUATION

We will conclude this section of our study with a list of exploratory questions that may help us examine our hearts with regard to our dependence upon food and other temporal pleasures. We must take care to cultivate such an intimate relationship with God that we find our greatest satisfaction in Him. We must always take heed that the "good gifts" in our lives do not become more important to us than the One who gave them!

1. Are you in bondage (excessive dependence) to food, entertainment, or temporal pleasure? Honestly examine yourself, and then write your thoughts.

_____

_____

_____

_____

_____

_____

_____

_____

_____

_____

2. Do you draw your comfort and satisfaction from food, companionship, temporal pleasures, or entertainment rather than from communion with God? Honestly examine yourself, and then write your thoughts.

_____

_____

_____

_____

_____

_____

_____

_____

_____

3. Is it easier for you to pass the day without communing with God in the Word and prayer than it is to miss a meal, be without your companions, or go without some form of entertainment? Honestly examine yourself, and then write your thoughts.

_____

_____

_____

_____

_____

_____

_____

_____

_____

_____

_____

CONCLUSION

Fasting can be a useful means of gaining mastery over our bodies and living in greater submission to the Lord. By fasting from food, entertainment, and other temporal pleasures, we can begin to see how important these things have become in our lives and how dependent we are upon them. If we become discontent, irritable, angry, or even despondent in the midst of fasting, we know that we have become dependent upon temporal delights rather than God. It is an ugly revelation; but it affords us an opportunity to repent, confess, and petition the throne of God for greater grace. Before breaking our fast, we should prayerfully seek the will of God regarding the use and enjoyment of food and other good gifts from God. Furthermore, we should determine how we might continue cultivating a deeper relationship with God and a greater dependence upon Him.

Chapter 9: Fasting Outward

Thus far, we have considered **fasting upward** and **fasting inward**. In this chapter, we will consider a final perspective: **fasting outward** for the advancement of Christ's kingdom in the world.

THE FOCUS

Outward fasting is concerned with everything related to the promotion of God's glory, the advancement of Christ's kingdom, and the redemption of the world. As Christians, our lives are to be consumed by these holy interests. We are called to live and labor for the glory of God and the benefit of all men. In light of the fallenness of this world and our own apparent weakness, our need for God is glaringly evident. For this reason, prayer is possibly the most significant activity in which the believer and the church can participate. In the face of an endless line of needs, the smallest of which is even beyond us, prayer becomes a primary labor; and in this labor, fasting may be employed.

In Chapter One, we reviewed an extensive list of the occurrences of fasting throughout the Scriptures. Through this, we learned that fasting was practiced for a variety of reasons; yet every instance had two things in common with the others: the impotence of man and the absolute necessity of God.

As we look upon our world in the twenty-first century, we see a nearly infinite number of needs that highlight our inability and require God's sovereign intervention. In such cases, prayer and fasting are entirely appropriate. In our culture of busyness and our tendency to take matters into our own hands, we must remember that seeking God should be our first response, not our last resort.

THE KINGDOM AND A HOLY DISCONTENT

The central and controlling passion of our Lord Jesus Christ is revealed in the Model Prayer, as recorded in Matthew 6:9-10:

> *Our Father who is in heaven,*
> *Hallowed be Your name.*
> *Your kingdom come,*
> *Your will be done,*
> *On earth as it is in heaven.*

In exactly the same manner, the Model Prayer should also reflect the central and controlling passion of our lives. We should long for God's name to be esteemed as holy above all others; for His kingdom to advance into every tribe, language, people, and nation; and for the entire universe to be brought into perfect obedience to His will. The fact that this has not yet occurred ought to create in us a holy longing or discontent that will not be remedied until the knowledge of the glory of God fills the earth as the waters cover the sea (Habakkuk 2:14).

The peace of God ought to rule in our hearts, regardless of circumstances; and we must learn to rest in His providence. At the same time, our passion for the kingdom ought to make us discontent, unsatisfied, and even grieved at the lack of worship given to God and the limited advance of the kingdom. This discontentment should lead us not only to more zealous activity, but also to perseverance in prayer. At times, this passion should be so strong that food is distasteful and temporal pleasures are forgotten. We must meet with God!

TENACIOUS PRAYING

God is the sovereign Lord of the universe who does according to His will in the host of heaven and among the inhabitants of the earth. No one can ward off His hand or say to Him, "What have you done?" He is not a God who can be manipulated or coerced by men (Daniel 4:34-35). However, throughout the Scriptures, this absolutely sovereign God commands His people to pray, call, ask, and even wrestle with Him in prayer. This is not a riddle to be solved but a mystery to be affirmed and a command to be obeyed. God calls us to persevere and prevail in prayer. We should not let Him go until He blesses us. We should give Him no rest until He has accomplished what He has promised! In the following, we consider just a few of the biblical texts that affirm such boldness in prayer.

1. In Matthew 7:7-8, we find three commands and three accompanying promises that demonstrate God's desire that we be importunate or tenacious in prayer. Identify these in the spaces below.

   a. *A_____, and it will be given to you (v.7).* What greater promise could God give to encourage us to pray? This promise is reminiscent of Psalm 81:10: "Open your mouth wide and I will fill it."

   b. *S_____, and you will find (v.7).* God promised the prophet Jeremiah, "You will seek Me and find Me when you search for Me with all your heart" (Jeremiah 29:13).

   c. *K_____, and it will be opened to you (v.7).* The truth conveyed is persistence—asking, seeking, and knocking until an answer is given.

   NOTES: Each of these commands is found in the present tense, indicating continuous action: "Go on asking, go on seeking, go on knocking..." A single prayer is not the key! Importunate, persisting, persevering, and tenacious prayer is the key! This will be further illustrated in the following text.

2. In Luke 18:1-8 is found one of the most important texts regarding the need to persist or persevere in prayer. Read the text until you are familiar with its contents; then answer the following questions.

a. *According to verse 1, what did Jesus command regarding prayer?*

(1) At A_____ times the believer O_____ to pray. The word "ought" is translated from the Greek verb **deí**, which communicates necessity. It shows that something is necessary, requisite, or essential. Similarly, it behooved or was necessary for (**deí**) Christ to suffer (Luke 24:46).

(2) And not to L_____ H_____. The phrase is translated from the Greek word **ekkakéō**, which means, "to faint, be weary, wear out, exhaust, or become spiritless."

b. *According to verses 2-5, how does the widow in the parable exemplify tenacious praying?*

_____

_____

_____

_____

_____

_____

_____

NOTES: A widow living in first-century Palestine was powerless to care for herself and had few or no resources (political, social, or economic) to gain a hearing in a court of law or to influence authorities to aid her in her plight. Although the judge in this parable is a man who neither fears God nor respects men (v.4), he is moved by the relentless pursuit of the widow who is literally **wearing him out** with her petitions. The phrase, "wear me out," comes from the Greek word **hupōpiázō**, which means, "to strike under the eye, buffet, beat, wear out, or treat severely."

c. *According to verses 6-8, how does Jesus apply the example of the widow to the prayer life of His disciples? How should we live in light of such promises?*

_____

_____

_____

_____

_____

_____

_____

NOTES: The point of the parable is this: if a cruel and compassionless earthly authority with only limited power can be moved to come to the aid of a powerless widow, how much more will our heavenly Father—whose lovingkindness is higher than the heavens (Psalm 103:11)—come to the aid of His beloved children when they seek Him?

d. _In the second half of verse 8, Jesus asks a very important question. What was the question, and what warning does it communicate to us as His disciples?_

_____

_____

_____

_____

_____

_____

_____

NOTES: The question is phrased literally, "…will He find **the** faith on the earth?" This is a warning to all Christians of every generation. Does the Lord find among us the kind of faith in His promises that moves us to tenacious praying? Or are we like those in Zephaniah 1:12, who were stagnant in spirit and said, "The Lord will not do good or evil"? Are we hopefully waiting for Christ's coming and our vindication? Or are we like the scoffers in the last days who say, "Where is the promise of His coming?" (II Peter 3:4)? The danger is not that God will be unfaithful to His promises, but that we will be unbelieving and faithless in prayer!

3. In Luke 11:5-10, we find still another amazing text regarding perseverance in prayer. Read the text until you are familiar with its contents, and then answer the following questions.

a. *What are the major truths being conveyed in verses 5-8?*

_____

_____

_____

_____

b. *According to verses 9-10, how does Jesus apply the truths of the previous illustration to His disciples? How should these truths be applied to our own prayer lives?*

_____

_____

_____

_____

_____

4. Isaiah 62:6-7 is one of the most amazing texts in all of the Scriptures. What does the text teach us about importunity or tenacity in prayer? How can it be applied to our prayer lives?

_____

_____

_____

_____

_____

_____

_____

NOTES: In the above text and in the parables of Luke 18:1-8 and Luke 11:5-10, we see a persistence that approaches annoyance. Although we must view these parables in the context of God's sovereignty and His dignity, we must not explain away their true intent: God calls us to persevering and relentless prayer. Such boldness honors God. Persevering prayer demonstrates genuine faith in the faithful character of God and in His power to accomplish what He has promised.

5. In the life of the patriarch Jacob, we find a wonderful example of tenacious praying. Read the account in Genesis 32:24-32; explain how this may be applied to the believer's prayer life.

_____

_____

_____

_____

_____

_____

NOTES: That God would allow and even invite such wrestling demonstrates His kindness and grace. Like the example of Jacob, our wrestling with God in prayer must reflect a biblical balance of boldness and great reverence.

PASSION, PRAYER, AND FASTING

As we grow in the grace and knowledge of God and in greater conformity to the image of His Son, we will become increasingly concerned about the matters of Christ's kingdom and increasingly burdened by them. We will be confronted by an almost infinite variety of needs: weakness in our own lives, suffering saints, struggling churches, unconverted friends, unevangelized nations, social injustice—the list goes on and on! As such profound matters are brought to our attention, we are commanded to take them to the Lord in prayer. If our hearts are any reflection of the texts we have studied in this chapter, we will not let God go until He has resolved the matter at hand or has revealed a greater measure of His will to us so that we might cease from asking and rest in His providence.

At these times, our passion for Christ's kingdom may become so intense that we "forget" or even "abhor" our food and other temporal pleasures (Psalm 102:4; 107:17-18). They can literally be "driven out" by our desire to see the advancement of Christ's kingdom. The matter at hand may be so weighty and the burden of our heart so great that we become blind to all temporal beauty and dead to all its delights. When these burdens are before us, we are oblivious to all else. We will not be put off. We will not be consoled. We will not let God go until He blesses. We will give Him no rest until the matter is resolved. As Naomi said of Boaz when he sought the redemption of Ruth, "The man will not rest until he has settled the matter today" (Ruth 3:18).

Such boldness may seem offensive or even irreverent to some. They may argue for God's sovereignty and explain that His decrees are fixed. They may even accuse us of attempting to manipulate deity. Yet in their sincere intention to protect God's dignity, they deny His Word. The language in the above paragraph comes directly from the Scriptures. It is God who commands such boldness. He is sovereign, and His decrees are fixed. He has predestined all things "according to His purpose," and He "works all things after the counsel of His will" (Ephesians 1:11). Yet He also tells us, "You do not have because you do not ask" (James 4:2). He commands us to give Him no rest with our petitions until He has fulfilled His promises (Isaiah 62:6-7). He implores us to ask, seek, knock, and find (Matthew 7:7-8). He gives us examples of men who would not let Him go until He blessed them (Genesis 32:24-32). He teaches us parables about unrelenting widows (Luke 18:2-7) and annoying neighbors (Luke 11:5-8). He does all of these things that we might seek Him boldly and tenaciously in prayer. Yet when the Son of Man comes again, will He find this kind of faith on the earth (Luke 18:8)?

Chapter 10: The Solemn Assembly

Part One: Solemn Assemblies in the Scriptures

In the Scriptures, fasting appears not only as a personal and individual discipline but also as a corporate or public practice. These times of public prayer and fasting are often referred to as **solemn assemblies**, **sacred assemblies**, or **holy convocations**.

Because Jesus warned not to publicize acts of devotion (Matthew 6:3-4, 6, 16-17), some have wrongly concluded that He prohibited all forms of public prayer and fasting. However, this is not the case. Throughout the Old Testament, there are countless instances of public prayer and fasting that were approved by God. In the New Testament, we find corporate prayer at the very outset of the early church (Acts 1:13-14) and in some of its most critical moments (Acts 4:23-31; 13:1-3).

Public prayer and, at times, fasting are not merely appropriate for the New Testament church—they should be encouraged! Based on the examples in the Scriptures, it is appropriate for a church to gather together in a solemn assembly for fasting and prayer during times of great need or crisis or at critical moments when the will of God for an extremely important matter must be discerned. It is also appropriate to gather the church together in a solemn assembly in order to celebrate the goodness of God with joy and feasting.

Although the term "solemn assembly" is not used in the New Testament, there are clear instances of the early church gathering together for corporate prayer. Furthermore, we must always remember the admonition of the Apostle Paul in Romans 15:4:

> *For whatever was written in earlier times [the Old Testament] was written for our instruction, so that through perseverance and the encouragement of the Scriptures we might have hope.*

To aid the student in his or her study, the following list has been provided with key biblical texts regarding the solemn assembly. Most of these texts make a direct reference to the solemn assembly, while others simply illustrate the practice.

I Samuel 7:5-6: The prophet Samuel gathered all Israel together at Mizpah to confess their sin and to seek the Lord's deliverance from the Philistines.

II Chronicles 7:9: King Solomon held a solemn assembly for all of Israel to dedicate the temple and to celebrate the goodness of God. The solemn assembly was accompanied by seven days of feasting with joy (see also Numbers 29:12).

II Chronicles 15:8-15: King Asa gathered together all the inhabitants of Judah to enter into a covenant with the Lord God to turn from their idolatry and seek Him with all their heart and soul.

II Chronicles 20:1-13: King Jehoshaphat gathered together all of Judah and proclaimed a fast to seek God's deliverance from the invading armies of Moab, Ammon, and the Meunites.

II Chronicles 23:16: The priest Jehoiada called all the peoples of Judah together to make a covenant among himself, the people, and the king—that they would be the Lord's people.

II Chronicles 34:31-33: King Josiah called together all who were present in Jerusalem and Benjamin to walk after the Lord and to keep His commandments with all their heart and soul.

Ezra 8:21-23: The priest Ezra called together the exiles traveling with him to Jerusalem in order to fast and to pray that God might protect them in the journey.

Ezra 10:1-12: A very large assembly from Israel gathered together with Ezra the priest to confess their sins and make a covenant with the Lord to separate themselves from the ungodly nations that dwelled in the land.

Nehemiah 9:1-3: Under the direction of Ezra the priest, the Israelites who had returned from exile separated themselves from all foreigners and assembled together to listen to the Word of God and to confess their sins with fasting and sackcloth.

Isaiah 1:10-15: Because of Israel's open rebellion and religious hypocrisy, the Lord had come to hate their sacrifices, religious festivals, and solemn assemblies.

Joel 1:14-15: Through the prophet Joel, God called together all the inhabitants of the land to go to the house of God and cry to the Lord, that divine judgment might be avoided.

Joel 2:12-17: Through the prophet Joel, God called all the people without exception to gather together in a solemn assembly to fast with true repentance, that divine judgment might be avoided.

Acts 1:4; 2:1: Prior to His ascension, Christ commanded the disciples not to leave Jerusalem but to wait for the outpouring of the Holy Spirit that was promised by the prophet Joel (2:28-32).

Acts 4:23-31: The disciples gathered together in the midst of persecution to ask the Lord for vindication and strength to witness with boldness.

Chapter 11: The Solemn Assembly

Part Two: The Call to a Solemn Assembly

As seen above, a solemn assembly may be called for various reasons. In what follows, we will consider two of the most common reasons found in Scripture: (1) to seek God's aid in a time of crisis, and (2) to repent of sin in order to divert God's judgment or discipline.

SEEKING GOD'S AID

In II Chronicles 20:1-30, King Jehoshaphat gathered together all of Judah and proclaimed a fast to seek God's deliverance from the invading armies of Moab, Ammon, and the Meunites. In this Old Testament event, the church can find much instruction and encouragement when it finds itself in times of crisis that are beyond its ability to resolve. Read II Chronicles 20:1-30 until you are familiar with its contents, and then complete the following exercises.

1. According to II Chronicles 20:1-2, what was the great crisis that confronted King Jehoshaphat and the people of Judah? What are some of the crises that might affect the church today and be appropriate reasons for calling a solemn assembly?

_____

_____

_____

_____

_____

_____

2. According to II Chronicles 20:3-4 and 20:13, how did Jehoshaphat and the people of Judah respond? How should the church respond when confronted with a crisis that is beyond its ability to resolve?

_____

_____

_____

_____

_____

_____

3. II Chronicles 20:5-12 records the prayer of King Jehoshaphat. In his prayer, we find four very important elements or characteristics that are worthy of imitation. Describe each element in your own words, and explain how each can be applied to the church today during an insurmountable crisis.

a. *God's Sovereign Rule (v.6)*

_____

_____

_____

_____

_____

_____

NOTES: All praying must be based on a belief in the omnipotence and absolute sovereignty of God.

b. *God's Promises (vv.7-9)*

_____

_____

_____

_____

_____

_____

NOTES: All praying must be founded upon God's promises. To doubt God's promises is unbelief, and to trust in what God has not promised is presumption. Both are sin!

c. *The Crisis (vv.10-11)*

NOTES: God knows our needs before we ask Him (Matthew 6:8), and He knows our crisis before it occurs (Isaiah 44:7-8). Nevertheless, we are to lay our needs before Him, present our case, and plead His promises.

d. *The People's Inability and Dependence (v.12)*

NOTES: Prayer is founded upon our twin beliefs in God's absolute sovereignty and our absolute impotence. Jesus confirmed God's blessings upon those who are poor in spirit and upon those who acknowledge their total dependence upon God and live accordingly (Matthew 5:3).

4. In II Chronicles 20:13-19, we read that God spoke to the people through Jahaziel, the son of Zechariah. What did God promise the people, and how did they respond to the Word of God? How might Jahaziel's preaching and the people's response be applied to the church today?

_____

_____

_____

_____

_____

_____

NOTES: Although we do not have specific prophecies regarding our problems, we do have the Word of God, which gives us countless promises regarding His faithfulness to care for His people and deliver them in times of trouble. The proclamation of God's character and His promises as they are set forth in the Scriptures are important elements in the solemn assembly.

5. According to II Chronicles 20:20-22, how did the people respond to God's directive to trust Him and not seek deliverance by the arm of the flesh? What can the church learn from their response?

_____

_____

_____

_____

_____

NOTES: The truth to be learned here is ***not*** that we should do nothing when faced with conflict. We must remember that God has also given us means to accomplish His ends. The truth to be learned is that we must trust in God and walk in obedience before Him. We must not lean on our own understanding or trust in our own strength and wisdom to deliver us. We should trust in the sufficiency of Scripture to guide us, and we should conform all our actions to its instructions and commands. We must not seek deliverance through compromise or through clever schemes.

6. According to II Chronicles 20:22-25, what was the result of Judah's trust in God? Did God deliver them? How can this truth be applied to the church?

_____

_____

_____

_____

_____

_____

NOTES: The deliverance described here is one of the most spectacular in all the Scriptures. However, through the ages of the church, there have been countless similar demonstrations of God's faithfulness and power to deliver His people when they had no possibility of delivering themselves. In the Scriptures and in the testimonies of God's faithfulness throughout the history of the church, we are given great encouragement to trust in the Lord and lean not on our own understanding (Proverbs 3:5-6). We are motivated to call upon Him and behold the strength of His arm to deliver.

7. In II Chronicles 20:26, we discover that another assembly was called after God's great deliverance of His people. What was the purpose of this assembly, and what does it teach us?

_____

_____

_____

_____

_____

_____

> **NOTES:** God's deliverance of His people should be appreciated and celebrated. The church that calls a solemn assembly to seek God's aid should also call a solemn assembly to praise Him after He gives it.

REPENTANCE AND RESTORATION

The book of Joel gives one of the most powerful and helpful descriptions of a biblical solemn assembly. Read Joel 1:14-15 and 2:12-17 until you are familiar with their contents. Then complete the following exercises.

1. Several events gave rise to the call for a solemn assembly: a locust plague (1:4-7), drought (1:9-12, 15-20), and warning of even more severe judgments (2:1-11). All these happened as a result of the sins of the people. A solemn assembly was called for the purpose of repentance and confession. How could this be applied to the church today?

_____

_____

_____

_____

_____

> **NOTES:** There are a number of reasons that a church might have need for corporate repentance: outstanding and widespread sin, failure to obey God in matters of church discipline, the growth of general apathy toward God, and so forth.

2. According to Joel 1:14 and 2:16-17a, who among the people of God was called to participate in the solemn assembly? How could this be applied to the church and its solemn assemblies?

_____

_____

_____

_____

_____

NOTES: The fact that all individual activities were to cease demonstrates the importance of the event. The children who attended the solemn assembly would receive an object lesson that they would never forget.

3. According to Joel 2:12-13a, how was true repentance manifested? How is the need for sincerity demonstrated in verse 13a? How can this be applied to the church and its solemn assemblies?

_____

_____

_____

_____

_____

_____

4. According to Joel 2:17, what was the primary purpose and petition of the solemn assembly? How can this be applied to the church and its solemn assemblies?

_____

_____

_____

_____

NOTES: The petition for deliverance demonstrates not only a concern for God's people, but also a concern for God's reputation among the nations. The sin of God's people often leads to the dishonoring of God's name (Romans 2:24).

5. What does Joel 2:13 tell us about the character of God? How is this an encouragement to those who seek Him with genuine repentance in the solemn assembly?

_____

_____

_____

_____

_____

_____

_____

_____

NOTES: Our hope for forgiveness and restoration does not rest upon our own virtue or merit, but upon who God is and what He has promised.

Chapter 12: The Solemn Assembly

Part Three: Practical Suggestions

This chapter of our study is taken directly from the booklet *The Solemn Assembly* by Richard Owen Roberts.[1]

1. **A Solemn Assembly is to be a time when all normal daily work is set aside.** This is clearly the instruction of Leviticus 23:34-36, Numbers 29:35, and Deuteronomy 16:8. While the overwhelming teaching of Scripture is in favor of hard work, it is absolutely clear that all work must be subjugated to spiritual concerns. Just as man is to labor six days—and six days only—and then rest on the seventh, so also man is to labor in times of spiritual and moral advance. But he is to set aside this normal daily work in order to seek the face of God during times of righteous judgment.

2. **A Solemn Assembly is a time when the entire body of people affected by God's righteous judgment is required to be in attendance.** This is clear in the several passages on Old Testament revivals, but nowhere more clear than in Joel where even the honeymooners had their honeymoon revoked, and the mother with an infant at her breast was required to be present (Joel 2:16). Part of the corporate sin that must be put away is that spirit of rebellion that exists in many professed Christians that causes them to believe that no spiritual leader can order them about. Such wicked sinners would do well to observe the severity of the denunciations against rebellion and stubbornness recorded in I Samuel 15:23.

3. **A Solemn Assembly is a time of fasting.** Rather than wondering concerning the physical significance of fasting, professed Christians would do well to face squarely the immediate spiritual importance. On a normal basis, we realize that the care of our bodies is a proper responsibility we assume before God. The care of ourselves is part of our normal service to God. But there are issues vastly more important than the care of our bodies. In fasting, a believing people acknowledge to God that the urgent concerns of the spiritual take precedence over the normal concerns of the physical. In short, fasting is an outward means of demonstrating a humility before God that acknowledges that the discovery of all those sins that have provoked His judgment and the putting away of them in an orderly corporate manner is of vastly greater consequence than the feeding of the body. There are times when the bodies of believers must be brought into subjection so that the overwhelming necessities of the spiritual may receive their due attention.

4. **A Solemn Assembly is a time for sacrifice.** Numerous Old Testament passages dealing with the Solemn Assembly make this clear (including Numbers 10:10 and 15:3). One of the

---

[1] Posted by special permission from the author and edited only for grammatical consistency. Copyright 1989 by Richard Owen Roberts; ISBN 0-926474-03-0; published by International Awakening Press, P.O. Box 232, Wheaton, IL 60189, USA. This material is also included as a chapter in a book edited by Mr. Roberts entitled, *Sanctify the Congregation: A Call to the Solemn Assembly and to Corporate Repentance*, published by International Awakening Press and available from Reformation Heritage Books.

greatest blessings God has given to mankind is the gift of time. What sacrifice could be more significant than the sacrifice of time in order to participate fully in God's commanded method of reversing a righteous judgment against a church or nation?

5. **A Solemn Assembly is of protracted duration.** While most professed Christians may content themselves with hour-long "worship" services, the call to a Solemn Assembly is a call to a greatly elongated meeting. In many of the passages where Solemn Assemblies are described, the assembly met for days on end—even as long as seven or fourteen days. On other occasions, however, it would appear that a full day was sufficient. In II Chronicles 7:8-9 it is noted that the feast was observed for seven days and then on the eighth day a solemn assembly was observed. It was at this Solemn Assembly that God said, "[If] My people who are called by My name humble themselves and pray and seek My face and turn from their wicked ways, then I will hear from heaven, will forgive their sin and will heal their land" (verse 14). No Solemn Assembly would be worth the name that did not allow at least an entire day for the great tasks of humiliation, prayer, repentance and seeking God's face.

6. **A Solemn Assembly is a season of earnest prayer.** Churches in general allot altogether too little time for prayer. Enough time may be taken to present requests to God, but precious little time is given corporately for God to present requests to men. But not only should much time be given to prayer at a Solemn Assembly, much time in prayer should be given in preparation for a Solemn Assembly. If the Solemn Assembly is to be held throughout the day on Saturday, the people of a church would do well to give considerable time to prayer throughout each day of the preceding week in preparation for the day itself.

7. **A Solemn Assembly is a mandatory occasion for corporate repentance.** In preparation for this, a catalogue of sins to be corporately confessed and put away should be prepared in advance. Some churches have solicited the involvement of the entire congregation in this catalogue. Various entities within the fellowship have been asked to prepare lists of the offenses against both God and man that they know the church has never corporately put away. The leaders have then gone over these lists and compiled them into a catalogue. The intent is not to manufacture wrongs but to seriously investigate any and all matters that might have contributed to the righteous judgment.

8. **A Solemn Assembly is an opportunity for Spirit-anointed preaching of the searching truths of Scripture to deeply touch afresh the lives of God's people.** In Solemn Assemblies where only a single day is devoted, it is not uncommon to have at least one or possibly two such sermons specifically aimed at the issues of the day and assisting the people in fulfillment of the responsibilities and grasping the opportunities the day presents.

9. **A Solemn Assembly is a most wonderful opportunity for children to see their parents and elders demonstrating Christianity at its deepest corporate levels.** Since the entire family is summoned, the youth and older children have a very special privilege of being deeply touched by the solemnities of the day. In some churches, outside baby-sitters have been hired to look after infants and the smallest children so that parents can devote their full attention to the work of the day.

10. **A Solemn Assembly gives God an opportunity to respond to His people at a level He cannot possibly do when they are living in neglect of His Word or in direct violation of His commandments.** Historically, God has responded to Solemn Assemblies by sending fresh waves of blessings into both the personal and corporate lives of believers; and, on some occasions, even glorious revivals have resulted. One of the most amazing instances of this is the Revival of the General Assembly in the Church of Scotland in 1596.

Chapter 13: Warnings and Promises

In our consideration of fasting, it is imperative that we consider two important themes: the rewards and the warnings associated with fasting. In the Scriptures, we find both promises and examples of God rewarding those who fast. However, we must be careful **not** to see fasting as a means of **manipulating** God or of **earning** His favor and blessing. In the Scriptures, we also find severe rebukes and even judgments upon those whose fasting is marked by self-centeredness, hypocrisy, and rebellion. In light of these truths, we must have a biblical understanding of both the rewards and warnings associated with fasting.

WARNINGS AND PROMISES FROM CHRIST

Matthew 6:16-18 is the most complete discourse in the Scriptures regarding fasting. In this text, Jesus gives great warnings alongside promises of reward. Read the text until you are familiar with its contents, and answer the following questions.

1. In Matthew 6:16, what name does Jesus give to those who practice fasting with impure and self-centered motives?

   a. H_____. The name is translated from the Greek word **hupokritês** and literally refers to an actor or thespian. Figuratively, it refers to a person who pretends to be something other than he truly is, or a person who masks or hides his true self. Christ reserved His most scathing rebukes for those who practiced religious hypocrisy (Matthew 15:7-9; 23:13-15, 23, 25, 27, 29; 24:51).

2. According to Matthew 6:16, how do the hypocrites fast, and what is their motive?

   _____

   _____

   _____

   _____

   _____

NOTES: The phrase "gloomy face" comes from the Greek adjective **skuthrōpós**, which can also be translated, "sad or sullen." The sad look of the hypocrite did not come from the heart but was put on like a mask. The word "neglect" is translated from the Greek word **aphanízō**, which means, "to disfigure or ruin." The hypocrite purposely neglected his appearance. Outward expressions of fasting, such as the wearing of sackcloth and the covering of oneself in ashes, are found throughout the Scriptures (Esther 4:1, 3; Isaiah 58:5; Jeremiah 6:26; Daniel 9:3; Jonah 3:6; Matthew 11:21; Luke 10:13). The practice is not condemned when observed with true humility and sincerity, but the hypocrites followed such practices in order to be seen by men and to receive their praise.

3. In Matthew 6:16, Jesus declares that the hypocrites who desire the glory of men will receive their reward in full. What does Jesus mean? Why is that not good news?

_____

_____

_____

_____

_____

_____

NOTES: The religious hypocrite fasts to receive the praise of man and has little genuine concern for a right relationship with God. Thus, God gives the hypocrite exactly what he desires. He receives man's praise but remains estranged from God. He receives his reward in full, gaining for himself man's praise and God's condemnation.

4. According to Matthew 6:17-18, how is the fasting of Christ's disciples to differ from that of the hypocrites? How does our obedience to Christ's directive demonstrate our sincerity?

_____

_____

_____

_____

_____

NOTES: The anointing of the head was not a daily practice but was reserved for joyful or celebratory occasions. As the hypocrite took pains to appear to be fasting, the sincere believer should take pains to appear not to be fasting. It is important to recognize that this teaching does not invalidate public or corporate fasting that is found and approved throughout the Scriptures. Christ is dealing with the intentions or motives of the heart. Important questions we might ask ourselves are, "For whom are we fasting?" and "By whom do we long to be seen and rewarded?"

5. According to Matthew 6:18, what is promised to those who seek God through sincere fasting? What does it mean?

_____

_____

_____

_____

_____

_____

_____

NOTES: The idea of fasting for reward may seem trite or even selfish. However, the same promise is made with regard to the giving of alms and prayer (6:3-4, 6). It is not the intention of Jesus to represent God as someone who can be manipulated into dispensing rewards by prayer, fasting, or other works of piety. However, we must not deny the truth that God has promised to provide for His people and bless those who seek Him by faith. We can glean two great truths from this text. **First**, works of piety flowing from sincere, Godward motives demonstrate our right relationship with God—He is our Father. **Second**, it is pleasing to God when His people come to Him believing that He is and that He is the rewarder of those who seek Him (Hebrews 11:6).

WARNINGS AND PROMISES FROM ISAIAH

Isaiah 58:1-12 provides the most powerful treatment of fasting in the Old Testament. Its stern warnings and splendid promises provide wise direction and hope to all who would seek the Lord. Read the text until you are familiar with its contents. Then answer the following questions.

1. In Isaiah 58:1, God commands the prophet Isaiah to declare the transgressions of His people. These transgressions are summarized below from the verses that follow. Basing your thoughts on each text, describe these transgressions; explain how they can have a negative impact on the believer's communion with God.

   a. **SPIRITUAL BLINDNESS AND HYPOCRISY** – Verse 2: "Yet they seek Me day by day and delight to know My ways, as [if they were] a nation that has done righteousness and has not forsaken the ordinance of their God. They ask Me for just decisions, they delight in the nearness of God."

   _____

   _____

   _____

   _____

   _____

   _____

   _____

   NOTES: The phrase, "as a nation that has done righteousness," is better translated, "**as if they were** a nation that has done righteousness." The people of Israel could not see their sin, and they sought God **as if they were** a nation that was walking in obedience to God.

   b. **UNRIGHTEOUSNESS** – Verses 3b-4a: "Behold, on the day of your fast you find your desire, and drive hard all your workers. Behold, you fast for contention and strife and to strike with a wicked fist."

   _____

   _____

   _____

   _____

_____

_____

_____

_____

> **NOTES:** All sorts of sins are revealed in these brief statements. It is important to note that to sin against others, especially against the people of God, is to sin against God Himself. Because of such sin, God withholds His fellowship and blessing. Fasting is of little effect if those who are fasting continue in unrighteousness.

2. In Isaiah 58:3, Israel asks, "Why have we fasted and You do not see? Why have we humbled ourselves and You do not notice?" According to verses 4-5, what is God's response to their questions? How can this admonition be applied to the believer and church today?

_____

_____

_____

_____

_____

_____

_____

_____

_____

> **NOTES:** External devotion without internal reality and practical obedience is strongly condemned throughout the Scriptures. The people were like the Pharisees whose devotion was external (Matthew 23:27), who made long prayers as a pretense (Matthew 23:14), and who fasted to be seen by men (Matthew 6:16).

3. According to verses 6-7 and verses 9b-10, what must accompany Israel's fasting so that it might be pleasing to God? How can these truths be applied to the believer and the church today?

_____

_____

_____

_____

_____

_____

NOTES: The wider application to these divine demands is that those who call upon the Lord in prayer and fasting so that He might do righteousness on their behalf must also do righteousness on behalf of others—especially to those of the household of God (Galatians 6:10).

4. According to Isaiah 58:8-12, what does God promise His people who call upon Him with sincere hearts and seek to live according to His righteous commands?

_____

_____

_____

_____

_____

_____

NOTES: Regardless of Israel's past sins, God promises them pardon, deliverance, and restoration.

WARNINGS FROM ZECHARIAH

Zechariah 7:1-14 contains another powerful admonition regarding fasting that is similar to that found in Isaiah 58:1-12. In this text, we will discover several truths (warnings) that can be applied to all who would seek the Lord. Read the text until you are familiar with its contents, and answer the following questions.

1. According to Zechariah 7:5-6, what was God's primary complaint regarding Israel's practice of fasting and their entire lifestyle? What is the application for the believer and the church today?

_____

_____

_____

_____

NOTES: Israel's religious devotion and lifestyle were driven by self-interest rather than concern for the honor of God and the well-being of others (Zechariah 7:9-10). The self-centeredness in which they lived was reflected in their fasting. They did not eat or drink for the glory of God (I Corinthians 10:31), and they did not fast for His glory.

2. According to Zechariah 7:8-12a, what were some of Israel's other sins that made their fasting unacceptable to God? What is the application for the believer and the church today?

_____

_____

_____

_____

_____

NOTES: Two of Israel's greatest sins were social injustice and a refusal to hear the Word of God as His prophets proclaimed it.

3. According to Zechariah 7:12b-14, what was the outcome of Israel's rebellion? What is the application for the believer and the church today?

_____

_____

_____

_____

_____

_____

_____

NOTES: Not even the most intense religious activity can save a person or a nation from judgment if they refuse to turn from their rebellion against God.

Chapter 14: Observations and Cautions

Fasting is a biblical practice that is appropriate for the New Testament believer and for New Testament churches. However, due to the extreme beliefs and practices associated with fasting throughout the history of the church, it is necessary that we hold tightly to the Scripture's teaching on the matter. We must not go beyond what is written or base our doctrine and practice on mere inference. The following is a list of biblical observations of fasting and necessary words of caution.

1. **Fasting is a biblical discipline that was practiced in both the Old and New Testaments.** Although fasting with impure motives was strongly condemned,[2] sincere fasting was commended and often rewarded.[3]

2. **In the Scriptures, fasting is practiced for a variety of reasons.**

    a. *DURING OR PRECEDING AN EVENT OF GREAT SIGNIFICANCE TO THE KINGDOM* – Moses fasted when receiving the Law (Exodus 24:12-18); Christ fasted prior to His testing and public ministry (Matthew 4:1-3); the disciples fasted prior to the beginning of the great missionary movement from Antioch (Acts 13:1-2).

    b. *INTERCESSION TO AVERT GOD'S JUDGMENT* – Moses interceded for rebellious Israel (Exodus 34:27-28); David asked God to spare his son whom God had struck with terminal illness (II Samuel 12:15-23); God commanded Israel to repent with fasting to avert coming judgment (Joel 1:14-15; 2:12-17); the Ninevites repented of their wickedness and fasted so the Lord might turn away the calamity He had declared against them (Jonah 3:4-10).

    c. *REPENTANCE AND CONFESSION* – Israel fasted with repentance at Mizpah (I Samuel 7:6-8); the wicked King Ahab humbled himself with fasting and was pardoned (I Kings 21:20-29); Nehemiah fasted as he confessed the sins of Israel and pleaded with God for mercy (Nehemiah 1:3-10); Israel fasted in a Solemn Assembly to hear God's Law and confess their sins (Nehemiah 9:1-3); Daniel fasted as he confessed his sin and the sin of his people (Daniel 9:3-20); God commanded Israel to repent with fasting to avert coming judgment (Joel 1:14-15; 2:12-17); the Ninevites repented of their wickedness and fasted that the Lord might relent concerning the calamity He had declared against them (Jonah 3:4-10).

    d. *DELIVERANCE* – Israel fasted for deliverance from the Philistines at Mizpah (I Samuel 7:6-8); King Jehoshaphat and Judah fasted for deliverance from the Moabites, Ammonites, and Meunites (II Chronicles 20:1-4); Ezra and the exiles fasted for God's protection on their journey to Jerusalem (Ezra 8:21-23); Nehemiah fasted for the deliverance of the remnant in Jerusalem who were suffering reproach and distress (Nehemiah 1:3-

---

[2] I Kings 21:9-13; Isaiah 58:3-5; Matthew 6:16; Luke 18:9-14
[3] Exodus 34:27-28; Judges 20:26-28; I Samuel 1:6-11; 7:6-8; I Kings 21:20-29; II Chronicles 20:1-4; Ezra 8:21-23; Nehemiah 1:3-4; 9:1-2; Esther 4:16; Daniel 6:16-19; 9:3-20; Jonah 3:4-10; Matthew 6:17-18

4); Queen Esther and the Jews in Susa fasted for deliverance from Haman's plot to exterminate the Jews (Esther 4:16); King Darius fasted for the deliverance of Daniel from the lions' den (Daniel 6:16-19).

e. *INQUIRIES REGARDING GOD'S WILL* – Israel fasted as they asked for God's direction in war (Judges 20:26-28); Daniel fasted as he asked for wisdom to understand the prophecies concerning Israel's future (Daniel 9:2-3, 20-23).

f. *SEEKING GOD FOR SPECIFIC ANSWERS TO PRAYER* – Hannah fasted as she asked for a son (I Samuel 1:6-11); David fasted as he asked God to spare his son whom God had struck with a terminal illness (II Samuel 12:15-23); Ezra and the exiles fasted as they asked for God's protection on their journey to Jerusalem (Ezra 8:21-23); Nehemiah fasted as he petitioned God to give him favor in the eyes of King Artaxerxes (Nehemiah 1:3-4, 11; 2:1-8); David fasted for the sake of those who were sick and needy (Psalm 35:13-14).

g. *MOURNING* – The men of Jabesh-gilead fasted as they mourned the death of Saul and his sons (I Samuel 31:11-13); David and his men fasted as they mourned the death of Saul, his sons, and those of Israel who had fallen in battle (II Samuel 1:11-12).

h. *ZEAL FOR GOD* – David wept and fasted because of his zeal for the things of God and because of the godless who reproached God's name (Psalm 69:9-10).

i. *SERVING OR MINISTERING TO GOD* – The prophetess Anna served God day and night in the temple with fasting and prayer (Luke 2:36-38); the disciples ministered to the Lord with fasting in Antioch (Acts 13:1-3).

j. *THE ORDINATION OF MINISTERS* – Although not commanded, the Scriptures mention fasting with reference to the ordination of missionaries (Acts 13:2-3) and elders (Acts 14:23).

3. **Fasting is an outward expression of the inward realities of humility, brokenness, fear, longing, mourning, and inability.** It is a spontaneous and heartfelt reaction to an extraordinary crisis, need, or desire. It occurs when the believer has to have God's forgiveness, deliverance, aid, comfort, wisdom, and presence at any cost. The believer literally "forgets" or "abhors" his food because of the affliction of his soul resulting from sin, longing, or need (Psalm 102:4; 107:17-18). The believer fasts because of an extreme delight in God that eclipses all temporal desires (Psalm 4:7; 27:4; 34:8; 42:1-2; 63:1; 73:25-26). There is no biblical mandate or support for practicing fasting as a mere procedure, regimen, scheduled program, formula, or method.

4. **Fasting was never intended as a religious ritual, a mark of piety, or a spiritual discipline to be routinely practiced.** There was only one day specifically set aside for fasting in the Old Testament—the Day of Atonement (Leviticus 16:29-31: "humble your souls"). The fasts on the fourth, fifth, seventh, and tenth months were established by the Jews during the exile (Zechariah 7:1-7; 8:19). By the time of Christ, the Pharisees had set days of fasting that they considered to be requirements of true piety (Luke 18:11-12; Matthew 9:14), but Christ condemned them as hypocritical (Matthew 6:16). It is lamentable that many early and medieval churches returned to the error of the Pharisees by making fasting an ordered ritual and a mark of genuine Christian piety.

5. **Jesus distinguished between the old order of fasting, which was practiced by the Pharisees and the disciples of John the Baptist, and the new order of fasting, which would be practiced by His disciples.**[4] Unlike the empty ritual of the Pharisees, the fasting of Christ's disciples would be born out of a heartfelt passion and longing for God. Unlike the fasting of John's disciples, Christ's disciples would not fast as those who were awaiting redemption but as those who had already experienced it!

6. **Although Jesus assumed that His disciples would fast, the New Testament contains no direct commandment or admonition to fast.**[5] Although fasting should be taught and even encouraged at times, it should not be required, commanded, declared compulsory, or set forth as a mark of spirituality. To do so is to return to the error of the Pharisees and the medieval church.

7. **It is heresy to "advocate abstaining from foods which God has created to be gratefully shared in by those who believe and know the truth."**[6] Furthermore, the Scriptures teach that believers are free with regard to the observance of days and eating: "He who observes the day, observes it for the Lord, and he who eats, does so for the Lord, for he gives thanks to God; and he who eats not, for the Lord he does not eat, and gives thanks to God" (Romans 14:6).

8. **The early church practiced fasting in the book of Acts.**[7] However, its infrequent appearance in Acts and the lack of specific New Testament instruction indicate that fasting was not routinely practiced. As many scholars have pointed out, a more accurate picture of the early church is found in Acts 2:42-47. Furthermore, it should be recognized that in the accounts of the two greatest prayer meetings in the book of Acts, fasting is not mentioned (Acts 1:12-2:4; 4:23-31).

9. **Although fasting was practiced prior to the commissioning of Paul and Barnabas and the ordination of elders in Asia Minor, it is not specifically commanded or implied to be a requirement.**[8] Jesus spent the night in prayer prior to choosing the twelve apostles, but no mention is made of fasting (Luke 6:12). There is no mention of fasting in the Apostles' selection of Matthias (Acts 1:23-26) or the seven (Acts 6:1-6). Paul gives no instruction to Timothy or Titus with regard to fasting in the selection and ordination of elders or deacons (I Timothy 3:1-15; Titus 1:5-9).

10. **Apart from Christ's brief instruction about fasting in Matthew 6:16-18, the Scriptures do not give us specific or detailed instruction about when or how to fast.** Most of our knowledge of fasting comes from narratives, examples, and prophetic reproaches and promises. In light of the scarcity of direct instruction regarding fasting, biblical fasting will be greatly dependent upon a mature understanding of the full counsel of God as it is revealed in the Scriptures (Romans 12:2) and upon a proper discernment of the leadership of the Holy Spirit (Psalm 32:8; Romans 8:14).

11. **It is exegetically inappropriate to raise fasting to the same level of importance as prayer.** The New Testament is permeated with a multitude of commands and instructions regard-

---

[4] Matthew 9:16-17
[5] Matthew 6:16; 9:14-15
[6] I Timothy 4:3
[7] Acts 13:2; 14:23
[8] Acts 13:1-2; 14:23

ing prayer. Believers are commanded to pray and are given extensive instruction regarding prayer. Such commandments and instructions about fasting are almost entirely absent in the Gospels and the Epistles.

12. **Prayer and fasting are sometimes combined in the Scriptures.**[9] However, there is no valid biblical argument for believing or teaching that fasting makes prayers more effective. Although there are many instances in which God answers the petitions of those who fast (Matthew 6:17-18), fasting does not guarantee answered prayer—God did not heal David's son (II Samuel 12:15-23).

13. **Fasting may be regarded as a help in spiritual warfare.** However, one should draw this conclusion from the overall teaching of Scripture on the matter and not from any single text (such as Mark 9:29—"So He said to them, 'This kind can come out by nothing but prayer and fasting'").

14. **Fasting may be an aid in disciplining the body and making it subservient to the will of God.**[10] However, any tendency toward ascetic practices and severe treatment of the body must be immediately and soundly rejected (Colossians 2:23).

15. **Any spiritual benefits derived from fasting can be rendered null by sin.** God rejected Israel's fast because it was not accompanied by repentance unto good works (Isaiah 58:1-14). The people from Jerusalem and the cities of Judah proclaimed a fast and listened as the scroll of Jeremiah was read. However, God's warning was not heeded (Jeremiah 36:20-26). The Pharisees fasted twice a week yet received no reward because of their hypocrisy and desire for self-glory (Matthew 6:16; Luke 18:9-14).

16. **There is a great need for biblical and practical wisdom regarding fasting.** This is especially true with regard to the length and intensity of fasting. Prolonged fasting may lead to physical weakness (Psalm 109:24). The fasts in which Moses and Elijah went forty days and nights without food or water (Exodus 34:28; Deuteronomy 9:9, 18; 1 Kings 19:8) were supernatural fasts that should not be attempted. A healthy individual may survive forty days without food but cannot survive more than three days without water. Those who have specific health conditions (such as heart problems, diabetes, pregnancy, and others) should consult a physician.

---

[9] I Samuel 7:5-6; II Samuel 12:16, 21-23; II Chronicles 20:3, 5; Ezra 8:21-23; Nehemiah 1:4; 9:1; Isaiah 58:6, 9; Jeremiah 14:12; Daniel 9:3; Luke 2:37; Acts 13:2-3; 14:23
[10] I Corinthians 9:24-27

Appendix: Practical Guidelines for Fasting

To conclude our study on fasting, we will consider a brief but important list of practical insights regarding the practice of fasting.

CONSULTING A PHYSICIAN

Limited fasting is not dangerous for a normal, healthy individual. However, expectant mothers and those with medical conditions should consult a physician before attempting a fast. It is not spiritual to put the Lord your God to the test (Matthew 4:7).

PHYSICAL DEMANDS ON THE BODY

1. **Fasting can take a toll on the body.** David declared, "My knees are weak from fasting; and my flesh has grown lean, without fatness" (Psalm 109:24).

2. **Second only to oxygen, water is the most important component of human life.** Water makes up 70-75% of a human's total body weight and approximately 90% of a person's blood. For this reason, the body needs to intake approximately 64 ounces of water daily. In extreme cases, people have survived without water for one week, but bodily functions begin to shut down after only a few days. There are a few supernatural fasts in the Scriptures (Exodus 34:28; Deuteronomy 9:9, 18; I Kings 19:8) in which there was no intake of water for forty days. Such fasts are **not** advised.

3. **After oxygen and water, healthy solid food is the third most important component to life.** Although food is set aside during most fasting, it is not because food is unspiritual or evil. The Scriptures teach that God created food to be gratefully shared in by those who believe and know the truth (I Timothy 4:3).

4. **Although fasting may cause physical discomfort, this is not the purpose of fasting.** Like food, the body was created by God and is good. Ascetic practices have no place in biblical fasting. The Scriptures warn that severe treatment of the body has no value against fleshly indulgence (Colossians 2:23).

BEFORE, AFTER, AND DURING A FAST

1. **A person who maintains a healthy diet and lifestyle will find it much easier and more enjoyable to fast.**

2. **It is a grave error both spiritually and physically to binge or eat a heavy meal before or after a fast.** Such eating not only defeats the purpose of the fast but also will result in discomfort during and after the fast.

3. **During a fast, it is extremely important to drink an adequate amount of water—at least sixty-four ounces each day.**

4. **During the first few days of a fast, it is not uncommon to experience light-headedness and even slight nausea due to toxins leaving the body.** Toxins accumulate in the body due to unhealthy eating habits. However, if these symptoms continue, it is wise to cease fasting and consult a physician.

KINDS AND LENGTHS OF FASTS

1. **In the Scriptures, we find different kinds of fasts.** These include: supernatural fasts without food or water for forty days (Exodus 34:28; Deuteronomy 9:9, 18; I Kings 19:8), total abstinence from food and water for three days (Esther 4:16), abstinence from food for forty days (Matthew 4:1-2), abstinence from delicacies while maintaining a basic diet (Daniel 10:3), and fasting in sackcloth and ashes (I Kings 21:27; Nehemiah 9:1; Psalm 35:13).

2. **In the Scriptures, we find different lengths of fasts.** These include: sunrise to sunset (Judges 20:26; I Samuel 14:24; II Samuel 1:12; 3:35), three days (Esther 4:16), seven days (I Samuel 31:13), three weeks (Daniel 10:3), and forty days (Exodus 34:2, 28; Deuteronomy 9:9, 18; I Kings 19:8; Matthew 4:1-2).

3. **The Scriptures prescribe no specific length for fasting.** For those who are just beginning to fast, it is wise to start small and gradually increase as desire and wisdom dictate. A believer may begin by fasting for one meal and using that time to seek the Lord in prayer. He may then advance to a "half-day" fast or a "morning to evening fast" and then increase as desire, biblical wisdom, and the Holy Spirit may dictate. Even within contemporary Christianity, fasting beyond one or two weeks is still practiced.

PERSONAL

FASTING

AND HUMILIATION

THOMAS BOSTON

PERSONAL **FASTING** AND HUMILIATION

Written by Thomas Boston (1676-1732).

Public domain. Originally published as *A Memorial Concerning Personal and Family Fasting and Humiliation* within *The Whole Works of Thomas Boston (Volume 11).* More information on the modernization and abridgement process is detailed by the editor, Forrest Hite, in "A Word from the Editor" in the introduction of this book.

Published by:

HeartCry Missionary Society
PO Box 7372
Roanoke, VA 24019

www.heartcrymissionary.com

Printed in the United States of America 2023

Unless otherwise noted, all Scripture quotations taken from the
New American Standard Bible®
Copyright 1960, 1962, 1963, 1968, 1971, 1972, 1973, 1975, 1977, 1995
by the Lockman Foundation. Used by permission.

Abridged, modernized, and edited by Forrest Hite

Chapter 1: An Overview of Personal Fasting and Humiliation

This reminder[11] is presented to both saints and sinners concerning religious fasts performed by a particular person in secret. Such fasts are indeed not the ordinary duties of all times—they are not required to be performed daily or at recurring times such as the duties of prayer, praise, and reading of the Word. They are, instead, extraordinary duties of certain times—they are to be performed occasionally, and the need for them depends entirely upon the call of providence (which is variable).

These duties are both described and charged to us in the Word of God. Therefore, when we have performed them, we must say, "We are unworthy slaves; we have done only that which we ought to have done" (Luke 17:10). We must despise the smallest thought of trying to gain or merit God's approval or favor by means of fasting!

The particular seasons for fasting are determined by providence; therefore, those who would fast must be keenly sensitive to God's call.[12] Otherwise, God may be calling for weeping and mourning, while they heedlessly indulge themselves in joy and gladness (Isaiah 22:12-13). This is a dangerous venture! "'Surely this iniquity shall not be forgiven you until you die,' says the Lord God of hosts" (v.14). Because of this, it is the most serious and tender Christians who are most readily found to be frequent in these exercises.

Fasting consists both of (1) an external and circumstantial part, and (2) an internal and substantial part.

THE EXTERNAL AND CIRCUMSTANTIAL PART OF FASTING

With regard to the external and circumstantial part, we will consider the following: **time**, **place**, and **abstinence**.

TIME

First of all, a proper time must be set apart for these duties. This is to be adjusted with Christian prudence, according to the person's situation.

As to the **time of day**, we find the saints in Scripture ordinarily kept their fasts by day. But we also have an instance of a personal fast kept by night in II Samuel 12:16: "David fasted and went and lay all night on the ground." I make note of this only to bypass the excuse of those who neglect this duty under the pretense of not being in control of their time. If the heart can be moved to fast, one will readily find some time or other to do so, whether by day or by night. It is recorded to the honor of the woman Anna that she served God "night and day with fastings and prayers" (Luke 2:36-37).

As to the **quantity of time**, I judge that one's need or situation ought not to be adjusted to the length of the fast; rather, the length of the fast ought to be adjusted to one's need or sit-

---

[11] Original word: "memorial"

[12] Original verbiage: They must be "religious observers of providence."

uation.[13] Esther's fast with her maidens, observed also by all the Jews in Shushan, lasted three days (Esther 4:16). We read of the "fast day" in Jeremiah 36:6. Sometimes, it appears, it was only part of a day that was spent in fasting, as in Cornelius's personal fast, which seems to have been over before the ninth hour (*i.e.* before three o'clock in the afternoon): "Four days ago I was fasting until this hour, and at the ninth hour I prayed in my house" (Acts 10:30 KJV). Daniel fasted and prayed until he received an answer "around the time of the evening offering" (Daniel 9:21), which was at the ninth hour.

Because of this, I believe that one should not be concerned[14] about the amount of time that is spent in these exercises; rather, his concern should be for the purpose of the fast. Indeed, I would argue that men often lay a snare for themselves by tying themselves to a certain quantity of time in such cases. It is sufficient to resolve that, according to our ability, we will take as much time as the work shall be found to require.

PLACE

A proper place is also to be chosen, where the person may perform the duty without disturbance from others. Both time and place are natural (not supernatural) circumstances of fasting—all places are alike now under the gospel; none are more holy than others. Men may pray anywhere, whether in the house or in the field, "lifting up holy hands" (I Timothy 2:8). Still, considering that personal fasting is a secret duty, it does require a secret place, as noted in our Savior's caution, "so that your fasting will not be noticed by men, but by your Father who is in secret" (Matthew 6:18).

ABSTINENCE

Abstinence is included in the very nature of fasting—abstinence from food and drink, abstinence from bodily pleasures, abstinence from worldly business. The Jews were unheeded by God in their fasting because they were finding pleasure and exacting their labors during their fasts (Isaiah 58:3). A time of religious fasting is a time "for a man to humble himself" (v.5) by denying himself even those lawful comforts and delights which he may freely use at other times. "They went into mourning, and none of them put on his ornaments" (Exodus 33:4). "So I gave my attention to the Lord God to seek Him by prayer and supplications, with fasting, sackcloth and ashes" (Daniel 9:3). "Do not deprive one another except with consent for a time, that you may give yourselves to fasting and prayer" (I Corinthians 7:5 NKJV).

The rule for abstinence from food and drink cannot be the same for everyone. Fasting is not itself a part of worship; it is a means to prepare and equip us for extraordinary worship. It is therefore to be used only as a **help** or **aid** in worship. Furthermore, it is certain that a given measure of it that would be helpful to that end for some would instead be a great hindrance to others. Therefore, those of a weaker disposition, whom total abstinence would restrain and render unfit for duty (the very opposite of a fast's purpose), are not called to fast at that rate; in their case, God's declaration takes precedence: "I desired mercy, and not sacrifice" (Hosea 6:6 KJV). Nevertheless, such persons can still use a partial abstinence and refuse to indulge themselves the use of food and drink with the same freedom as at other times—altering either the quantity or quality of them (or both). In doing so, they too may be "afflicted" (Leviticus 23:29). So Daniel in his mourning "did not eat any tasty food, nor did meat or wine enter [his] mouth" (Daniel 10:3).

---

[13] Original verbiage: "As to the quantity of time…the duty, I judge, is to regulate it, and not it to regulate the duty."
[14] Original word: "solicitous"

THE INTERNAL AND SUBSTANTIAL PART OF FASTING

The things mentioned above are but the outward shell of fasting; the internal and substantial part of it lies in the following spiritual exercises.

1. SERIOUS MEDITATION AND CONSIDERATION OF OUR WAYS. "Now therefore, thus says the Lord of hosts, 'Consider your ways!'" (Haggai 1:5). We are diligently to review our past life. During times of fasting, we should keep ourselves from conversing with the world, that we may more seriously examine our own hearts to discern the state of matters between God and us. "Let us examine and probe our ways" (Lamentations 3:40). We are to **search out** our sins, sorrowfully calling to remembrance the sins of our heart and life, while being as specific as we can. And we are to **search into** them, deeply considering the evil of them—(1) contemplating the light, love, mercies, and warnings we have sinned against; and (2) tracing these aggravations against God up to the sin of our nature, the poisoned fountain from which they all have proceeded. The more fully and freely we converse with ourselves about our sins, the more fit we will be to speak to God about them in confession and in pleading for pardon.

2. DEEP HUMILIATION OF SOUL BEFORE THE LORD. Under the Old Testament law, this was signified by the use of sackcloth and ashes. We ought to consider our ways until our soul is humbled within us; our heart is torn both with remorse and with regret and familiar[15] sorrow for sin, as an offence to a "gracious and compassionate" God (Joel 2:12-13); our face is filled with shame and embarrassment before Him in view of our spiritual nakedness, pollution, and defilement (Ezra 9:6); and our very self is loathed as vile and insignificant in our own eyes (Ezekiel 36:31; Job 40:4).

3. FREE AND OPEN CONFESSION OF SIN BEFORE GOD WITHOUT RESERVE. This is a very tangible part of the duty required of us in religious fasting. The consideration of our ways and humiliation of our souls mentioned above naturally produce this extraordinary confession of sin, an exercise most suitable for such an occasion. The Jews spent a fourth of the day confessing and worshiping (Nehemiah 9:3); and the angel who brought the answer to Daniel's supplications found him still praying and confessing his sin (Daniel 9:20-21). Truly, the humbled sinner has much to work through at this point[16]—(1) acting the part of an accuser against himself, recounting before the Lord his transgressions of the holy law, as much as he can remember; (2) acting the part of a lawyer, bringing to mind the specifics and the aggravating circumstances of the crimes; and (3) acting the part of a judge, both in justifying God in all the judgment He has brought upon him and in condemning himself as unworthy of the least of all His mercies and deserving to perish under eternal wrath.

4. REPENTANCE IN BOTH HEART AND LIFE. Repentance is the exercise of turning from sin to God; it is the natural result of deep humiliation and sincere confession. "Return to Me with all your heart, and with fasting, weeping and mourning" (Joel 2:12). We fast in vain if our love of sin is not turned into hatred, if our liking of sin is not turned into loathing, and if our cleaving to sin is not turned into a longing to be rid of it. We fast in vain if we do not fully purpose to resist any movement toward sin in our heart and any outbreaking of sin in our life. We fast in vain if we do not turn to God as our rightful Lord and Master and return to our calling as

---

[15] Original word: "kindly" (*i.e.* natural or involuntary)

[16] Original verbiage: "For here the sinner duly humbled has much ado…"

His servants. If we are truly repentant, we will turn from sin not only because it is dangerous and destructive to us; but also because it is offensive to God, dishonors His Son, grieves His Spirit, transgresses His law, and defaces His image. If we are truly repentant, we will cast away all our transgressions, both as one would cast away a hot coal because it burns him, and as one would cast away something filthy because it defiles and disgusts him. But with all of this, it must be remembered that the true way to deal with a hard heart and to bring it to this temperament is **belief in the gospel**. As ravenous birds of prey first fly upward and then come down on their victims, so we must first soar high in believing and then come down in deep humiliation, sincere and free confession, and true repentance. "They will look on Me whom they have pierced; and they will mourn" (Zechariah 12:10). The Scriptures describe God's promise of grace as a motive for our repentance and suggest that belief in this promise will move hardened hearts: "Now return to the Lord your God, for He is gracious" (Joel 2:13). One may work long and hard to repent; however, without this faith in God's promise, it is all in vain. Without faith "it is impossible" to please God (Hebrews 11:6); so without faith it is impossible to reach true humiliation, right confession, and sincere repentance—all of which are very pleasing to Him (Jeremiah 31:18-20). The law can bring an unbelieving sinner to the point of being horrified, but one will never become a natural mourner of sin except by the influence of the gospel.[17] When guilt stares one in the face, unbelief locks up his heart, as the bitter cold freezes water; but faith in the Redeemer's blood melts that ice, so that it flows in tears of godly sorrow. **Unbelief** will suggest harsh thoughts of God to a guilt-burdened soul, which will only alienate that soul more and more from Him, so that he cowers away from God in self-defense. But **belief** in the pardon that God has proclaimed will touch the heart of the rebel so that he casts himself at the feet of his Sovereign, willingly yielding himself to Him.

5. SOLEMN COVENANTING WITH GOD. This ought to be done aloud, with deliberate language. As a fast day is a day to "loosen the bonds of wickedness" (Isaiah 58:6), so it is a day for coming explicitly into the bond of the holy covenant: "They will go along weeping as they go, and it will be the Lord their God they will seek... They will come that they may join themselves to the Lord in an everlasting covenant that will not be forgotten" (Jeremiah 50:4-5). This covenant naturally follows after humiliation, confession, and repentance, through which our alliance with sin is broken. It consists of a solemn profession before the Lord (1) that we take hold of His covenant, believing on the name of His Son, both as the Savior of the world and as our Savior; (2) that—in and through Him—He will be our God, and we shall be His people; and (3) that we are content in our soul to take Him for our portion, as our Lord and Master, and to resign ourselves to Him only, wholly, and forever.[18]

6. EXTRAORDINARY PRAYER. We are to address our covenanted God with persistent[19] petitions, according to the particular purpose of our fast. The confession and the covenanting (as discussed above) are, of course, both to be done in prayer (see Daniel 9:4-15 and Nehemiah 9:6-38). Additionally, however, there must be prayers, supplications, and petitions made for the specific situation or need that has driven the person to fast. "But as for me, when they were sick, my clothing was sackcloth; I humbled my soul with fasting, and my prayer kept returning to my bosom" (Psalm 35:13). Indeed, the great purpose and design of such fasting is

---

[17] Original verbiage: "The unbelieving sinner may be brought to roar under law-horror; but one will never be a kindly mourner, but under gospel influences."

[18] See Psalm 16:2; Isaiah 44:5; 49:8; 56:6; John 1:12; and Hebrews 8:10 for more on this topic

[19] Original word: "importunate"

to help make the one who fasts more **motivated** and **equipped** to wrestle with God in prayer concerning the particular case which has burdened his heart. So the Ninevite king, burdened with the threat of destruction, ordered that "both man and beast be covered with sackcloth" and that men were to "call on God earnestly" (Jonah 3:8). The Ninevites were to cry in prayer for pity and mercy; and, so that they might be moved to greater fervency in these cries, it was commanded that they and even their beasts be covered with sackcloth. These circumstances—the cries of the desperate men, mixed with the cries of the uncomfortable and hungry beasts (Job 38:41)—would make the seriousness of that extraordinary mourning very great; and the hearts of men—every now and then pierced with the cries of the harmless animals—would be stirred up to a more earnest, fervent, and persistent pleading with God for mercy.

REVIEW QUESTIONS

1. What are the three external or circumstantial aspects of fasting listed by Boston?

_____

_____

_____

2. Choose one or two of the internal or substantial aspects of fasting that especially resonated with you. In your own words, describe the benefit of following said practice(s) during a fast.

_____

_____

_____

_____

_____

_____

_____

_____

Chapter 2: The Divine Warrant for Personal Fasting and Humiliation

Nothing can be called obedience to God unless it is derived from and directed by the revealed will of God—indeed, "self-made religion" is condemned by the Word (Colossians 2:23). In view of this fact, it should be the concern of all who would in faith perform the duty of fasting to know **who it is that warrants it**, so that they might be truly obedient. To shed light on this matter, that it might be bound to our conscience as a duty prescribed by God, let us contemplate the following things.

1. **Fasting is expected of God's people in God's Word, both directly and indirectly.**

   a. *It is directly expected in the Word.* "Be miserable and mourn and weep" (James 4:9). It is plain from the surrounding verses that these requirements were given to specific persons in the context of their personal situations (see verses 8 and 10). What was actually being required of them in these commands—namely, fasting and humiliation—would have been very clear to them, for this epistle was written to those Jews by nation who were "dispersed abroad" (James 1:1), and this is the very language of the Old Testament. Their prophets called them to the duty of fasting using the same manner of expression: "On exactly the tenth day of this seventh month is the day of atonement... you shall **humble your souls**"—that is, with fasting (Leviticus 23:27). "Is it a fast like this which I choose, a day for a man to **humble himself**?" (Isaiah 58:5). "Return to Me with all your heart, and with fasting, **weeping and mourning**" (Joel 2:12). Note that the **mourning** required in these texts differs from the **weeping**, as the **countenance** of mourners differs from their **tears** (Genesis 37:34; Ecclesiastes 3:4).

   b. *It is indirectly expected in the Word.* Considering that God has given us directions concerning fasting, it is natural to suppose that it is a duty that saints **will** in fact practice. Our Savior gives us directions about personal fasting: "Whenever you fast, do not put on a gloomy face as the hypocrites do, for they neglect their appearance so that they will be noticed by men when they are fasting. Truly I say to you, they have their reward in full. But you, when you fast, anoint your head and wash your face so that your fasting will not be noticed by men, but by your Father who is in secret; and your Father who sees what is done in secret will reward you" (Matthew 6:16-18). This indicates that fasting is indeed a duty that He has required, for it would be inconsistent with the holiness of God for Him to give directions regarding "self-made religion," which He condemns (see Matthew 15:9; Colossians 2:23; and Jeremiah 7:31).

2. **Fasting is promised in God's Word—namely, that the saints would perform this duty.** God clearly states in His Word that His people will participate in personal fasting. "I will pour out on the house of David and on the inhabitants of Jerusalem, the Spirit of grace and of supplication, so that they will look on Me whom they have pierced; and **they will mourn** for Him... and **they will weep bitterly** over Him... In that day **there will be great mourning** in Jerusa-

lem… **The land will mourn**, every family by itself…and their wives by themselves" (Zechariah 12:10-12). It is here promised that fasting and humiliation will in fact take place as an act of obedience among God's people. Furthermore, our Lord Jesus promised it of His disciples: "The days will come when the bridegroom is taken away from them, and then **they will fast**" (Matthew 9:15).

3. **Fasting is recommended in God's Word through the practice of the saints mentioned in Scripture.** It was, as we have already seen, practiced by **David**, a man after God's own heart (II Samuel 12:16; Psalm 35:13). It was practiced also by **Daniel**, a man greatly beloved (Daniel 9:3; 10:2-3). It was performed by the devout centurion **Cornelius** (Acts 10:30). It was a frequent exercise of **Paul**, the laborious apostle of the Gentiles (II Corinthians 11:27). All of these saints pleased God in their work; and it is our duty to walk in the footsteps of the flock, following their approved example.

4. **Fasting is encouraged in God's Word through the occasional duty of societal fasting and humiliation.** The reality of these public fasts will not, I presume, be questioned.[20] From these examples, we can glean the following encouragements for personal fasting and humiliation.

   a. *There is nothing in the nature of religious fasting and humiliation that is essentially public or that necessarily requires a group of people.* The preaching of the Word and the celebration of the sacraments naturally require society or community; therefore, they are not meant for one person alone in his closet. But this is not so with fasting. One may keep a fast alone just as well as he may pray, read the Scriptures, or sing praises alone. If God has appointed a duty, and He has not tied that duty to societies or assemblies or specific groups, then that duty belongs to every individual who is able to perform it.

   b. *The extraordinary occasions that call for the fasting and humiliation of an assembly in a public capacity apply also to individuals.* If a church or congregation is called on such occasions to fasting and humiliation, is not an individual called on such occasions to do the same? If abounding sin in a congregation or looming judgment on a nation requires solemn public fasting and humiliation, would not abounding sin in an individual or looming judgment on his soul require personal fasting and humiliation? Surely, every person ought to keep his own vineyard with the same diligence that the public vineyard is to be kept; if one does not do so, it will yield bitterness in the end (Song of Solomon 1:6).

   c. *Because large bodies move slowly, nations and congregations rarely respond quickly to God's call for a public response to a great crisis or need.* God's providential call for national or congregational fasting and humiliation often goes unheeded. In such instances, what should be the response of individual believers who do discern God's call at that time? Should they sit still and not answer the call **as they are able** (i.e. personally), because they cannot answer it **as they desire** (i.e. corporately)? Should they not instead keep personal fasts for the very causes for which others either cannot or will not keep public fasts? When God pleaded with the land of Egypt, those "among the servants of Pharoah who feared the word of the Lord" took action in response to His warning (Exodus 9:20), though the nation as a whole refused to repent.

---

[20] See Judges 20:26; Ezra 8:21-23; Joel 1:14; and Jonah 3:5-9 for examples

REVIEW QUESTIONS

1. According to Boston, why is it so important to know that God warrants fasting in His Word?

_____

_____

_____

_____

2. Name a passage from the Old Testament and a passage from the New Testament where fasting by God's people is expected, promised, recommended, or encouraged. What do such texts teach us about God's view of fasting in a proper manner?

_____

_____

_____

_____

3. What can we learn from biblical accounts of corporate or public fasting that can apply to our individual practice of this discipline? How should a believer respond when he or she sees a need for a solemn assembly (see pages 45-57) but is alone in that burden?

_____

_____

_____

_____

_____

Chapter 3: A Providential Call to Personal Fasting and Humiliation

The circumstances of an *individual* or those of his *church* or of his *neighbor* may each separately—and more so all of them together—elicit a providential call to personal fasting and humiliation. The prophet Daniel kept a personal fast on the church's account (Daniel 9:2-3), while David kept one on his neighbor's account (Psalm 35:13) and one on his own account (II Samuel 12:16).

God's children should consider that which is in His kingdom's interest to be in their own interest. Secret personal fasting for the sake of the kingdom is therefore highly commendable and, if done properly, very acceptable in the sight of God (Daniel 9:20-21).[21]

Communion with saints is a most beneficial thing. Two aspects of this which are helpful for us to take into account here are a communion of *burdens* (Galatians 6:2) and a communion of *prayers* (James 5:16), which are among the best cordials the travelers to Zion have on their way. For one to love his neighbor as himself—of which secret fasting on his neighbor's account is good evidence—is better than all burnt offerings and sacrifices (Mark 12:33). And whether it does his neighbor good or not, it will not fail, if done rightly, to return many benefits into his own bosom, according to the Psalmist's experience (Psalm 35:13).

Be that as it may, it is hardly to be expected that one would fast on the account of others if he has not yet done so on his own account. But surely, if professors of religion were more concerned about and engaged in their own spiritual wellbeing and progress, this duty of personal fasting and humiliation would not be so rare as it is. The Apostle Paul, who showed great concern over such things (Acts 24:16), was "in fastings often" (II Corinthians 11:27 KJV) and disciplined his body to bring it into subjection (I Corinthians 9:27).

GENERAL EVENTS THAT CALL FOR FASTING

There are three kinds of events that call for this extraordinary duty, when circumstances and providence permit.

Either, *first*, when there is any *special evil*—whether sin or its consequence—that is facing us, the church, or a neighbor for whom we have a special concern. There are some sins that leave such guilt on the conscience and such defilement on the heart and life that they call aloud, as it were, for fasting and humiliation in order to recover from their dismal effects. James 4:8-9 reads, "Draw near to God and He will draw near to you. Cleanse your hands, you sinners; and purify your hearts, you double-minded. Be miserable and mourn and weep; let your laughter be turned into mourning and your joy to gloom." Thus the Israelites, having become aware of the abominable idolatries into which they had fallen, gathered at Mizpah and "fasted on that day and said there, 'We have sinned against the Lord'" (I Samuel 7:6).

Likewise, when the reality of God's strong disapproval of our sin is displayed in the consequences His providence allows, it is time for us to roll ourselves in the dust in humiliation—and

---

[21] Original verbiage: "Zion's children should reckon her interest theirs; and as secret personal fasting for public causes, argues a truly public spirit; so it is highly commendable, and being rightly managed, is very acceptable in the sight of God (Daniel 9:20-21)."

humbling ourselves before Him with fasting is a helpful way to bring ourselves to this point.[22] Thus Nehemiah found himself called to fasting when he received information of the continued ruin of Jerusalem and the affliction that the returned captives were enduring (Nehemiah 1:3-4). Thus David and those with him found themselves called to fasting when hearing of the defeat of Israel and the death of Saul and Jonathan (II Samuel 1:12). And thus the people of Israel found themselves called to fasting when the Benjamites slew thousands of their own kindred in battle (Judges 20:26).

Or, **secondly**, when there is any **special peril** that is threatening or looming. Thus the inhabitants of Jerusalem, in imminent danger at the hands of their enemies, were providentially called to weeping and mourning, though they heeded it not (Isaiah 22:12-13). The Ninevites, however, fearing their impending destruction, did heed the call of providence (Jonah 3:4-9). So did David when God struck his child with sickness (II Samuel 12:15-16). Indeed, so did even Ahab when he heard Elijah's heavy message against him and his house (I Kings 21:27). As when the lion roars, it becomes us to fear; so when God's hand is lifted up, ready to strike, it is high time for us to humble and abase ourselves.

Or else, **thirdly**, when there is some **special mercy and favor** that is desired of the Lord. Thus Daniel, yearning for Israel's return from the Babylonian captivity, kept his fast (Daniel 9:1-3). Christians genuinely engaged in the pursuit of godliness will rarely (if ever) lack a response from God, whether immediate or delayed, to the specific desires they lay before His throne of grace. God sometimes causes certain mercies to fall into the laps of men even when they do not bring their needs or wants before Him. However, He will often have His own children come to Him to plead their requests many times before He grants them. The former receive their gifts only by means of common grace, and a curse may in time be revealed alongside the mercy. The latter are made to walk and hope in God's promises and are thereby not only blessed with the gifts but also sanctified through the process.[23]

PARTICULAR CASES THAT CALL FOR FASTING

In order to make the matter clearer, we will look at some examples that fall under these general headings. These primarily consider an individual's private circumstances, though in several instances they are also very applicable to the circumstances of his church or of his neighbor. Below are several particular cases that (when one discerns that his situation allows for it) call for personal fasting and humiliation.

1. **When, through a long track of sinning and careless walking, the state of one's soul is left quite in disorder and confusion.** "Tremble, you women who are at ease; be troubled, you complacent daughters; strip, undress and put sackcloth on your waist" (Isaiah 32:11). God's exhortation to such is certainly, "Thus says the Lord of hosts, 'Consider your ways!'" (Haggai 1:5). Lack of self-examination ruins many people. They deal with their souls as some foolish men deal with their businesses, running them without consideration until they have run them-

---

[22] Original verbiage: "In like manner, when the tokens of God's high displeasure are gone out in afflicting providences, it is time for us to roll ourselves in the dust; and so to accommodate our spirit and way to the dispensation, humbling ourselves before him with fasting."

[23] Original verbiage: "Christians exercised into godliness, will rarely, if ever, want their particular suits, and special errands unto the throne of grace. The same God, who makes some mercies fall into the lap of others, without their being at much pains about them, will give his own children many an errand unto himself for them, ere they obtain them, because they must have them in the way of the covenant; whereas they come to others only in the way of common providence, in which a blasting curse may come along with the mercy."

selves aground. But those who have ventured into a season of sin have need to take also a set time for mourning; for it is not to be expected that accounts that are long overdue will be cleared and adjusted with but a glance of one's eye. Oh, careless sinner, consider how matters stand between God and you—are you in a state ready for death and eternity? Is your soul not in a wretched condition? Are you not wasting away in your iniquity? Is not the state of your soul like that of the sluggard's vineyard, that "was completely overgrown with thistles; its surface was covered with nettles, and its stone wall was broken down" (Proverbs 24:31)? Oh, set yourself upon personal fasting and humiliation! Ordinary work is not sufficient to restore a long-neglected garden; it must be turned over completely. A little work may help the case of a garden that is regularly trimmed and treated; but this would not prove enough for yours, which has lain so long neglected.

2. **When one is under conviction and is considering reform.** During such a time did the sons of Israel fast (Nehemiah 9:1-2), and this had very good effects (10:28-29). Fasting is a good way to make men serious about reforming and to strengthen their resolutions, which otherwise may prove fruitless. Some men have convictions that come and go, which occasionally stir them to pray, but never bring them to a settled course of reformation of life. Their disease is too firmly established to be carried off so easily. But if they were wise enough to make these convictions a matter of solemn seriousness, setting some time apart for personal fasting and humiliation when conviction comes, they might by God's grace prevail in their endeavor to reform.

3. **When one's conscience is defiled with the guilt of some atrocious sin.** If national guilt of such a sin calls for national fasting, should personal guilt of the same kind not require personal fasting? Indeed, God calls men in such cases to be miserable, to mourn, and to weep (James 4:8-9). As strong diseases require strong remedies, so conscience-searing guilt requires deep humiliation, as in David's case (Psalm 51) and in Peter's (Matthew 26:75). This kind of guilt—that which deeply wounds and stings the soul and which defiles and ruins the conscience—may not appear as an enormous scandal for the world to see. But God is witness to secret sins, even to the sins of the heart; and men of tender consciences will be made sick at heart by such sins, even if they are hidden from all the world.

4. **When one would be glad to overcome a snare that has often entangled him and to have victory over a lust that has often mastered him.** Plenty of people have many good things that can be said about them, yet lack one thing; and that one thing is likely to stand between heaven and them, tarnishing all their good things (Mark 10:21). It is a wrong that they often resolve to amend, and they would gladly be rid of it. But whenever a new temptation comes and Satan attacks them at their weak point, down go all their resolutions, as suddenly as a tall pillar that snaps under a weight it cannot support, and they are hard and fast in the snare again. Oh, friends, this kind does not go out except by prayer and fasting (Matthew 17:21)! Therefore, set some time apart for personal fasting and humiliation on account of that specific snare, that you may wrestle with God in prayer about it. Do it over and over again until you prevail against it. Otherwise, that one thing may ruin you, and you will be condemned for it—not because you could not help it, but because you would not use the means appointed by God for relief against it.

5. **When one is under a "dead desertion."** By this I mean a case in which the Lord is departed from a man, the usual influences from heaven being withheld from him, but he is not affected or hurt much by this fact due to a spiritual deadness that has gripped him. Such was the case of the spouse in Song of Solomon 3:1: "On my bed night after night I sought him whom my

soul loves; I sought him but did not find him." And she made some extraordinary efforts to recover from it (vv.2-4)! The same appears to be the case of many with whom it was better in time past than it is now. God hides His face from them; heaven's benefits are rare and meager compared to former times; they are drained and slipping backward. Though they still go through religious motions, it has been long since they have had a token from the Beloved or felt communion with God. Oh, fast and pray for a recovery! Thus Israel did when, after they had been long deserted and affected very little by it, they began to lament after the Lord (I Samuel 7:2, 6). It takes a lot of work to restore that which idleness has damaged, like a neglected building that has fallen into decay. Though true grace can never be totally lost, it may be brought to a very low place.

6. **When one is under a "felt desertion."** By this I mean a case like the one above, except that the Lord's departure affects the man dearly—he feels its sting. "But Zion said, 'The Lord has forsaken me, and the Lord has forgotten me'" (Isaiah 49:14). This is a more hopeful case than the former, though it hurts deeply. "The spirit of a man can endure his sickness, but as for a broken spirit who can bear it?" (Proverbs 18:14). There are many bitter ingredients in it that make it a sorrowful case, exquisitely painful to the soul, like that of a "wife forsaken and grieved in spirit" (Isaiah 54:6). One who is under this desertion sees wrath in the face of God and in all his circumstances (Psalm 88:7-8). Both his senses and his emotions tell him, "Your prayers are shut out! This terror will destroy you!" (cf. Lamentations 3:8; Psalm 88:15-16). Under this kind of pressure, some very sober and sound persons have been unable to contain themselves—"I go about mourning without comfort; I stand up in the assembly and cry out for help" (Job 30:28). This felt desertion, whether in greater or lesser measure, has often been the fearful follow-up of dead desertion, as it was in the experience of the spouse (Song of Solomon 5:3-7). And it is a loud call to personal fasting and humiliation: "But the days will come when the bridegroom is taken away from them, and then they will fast" (Matthew 9:15).

7. **When one is oppressed by some outward affliction—whether in his body, relationships, name, position, or otherwise.** In such a case, "Job arose and tore his robe and shaved his head, and he fell to the ground and worshiped" (Job 1:20); and David's knees were "weak from fasting" (Psalm 109:24). A time of affliction is a special season for fasting and prayer. The Lord often lays affliction on his people in order to awaken them to their duty and show them its importance. "Humble yourselves in the presence of the Lord, and He will exalt you" (James 4:10)—this is how affliction sanctifies a person and (in due time) is removed. We should therefore be careful not to be like those who do not cry out to God when He brings affliction; rather, we should learn from Ben-hadad's servants, who, having been soundly defeated in battle, put on sackcloth and went out as humble supplicants to the Israelite king who had vanquished them (I Kings 20:31).

8. **When one is threatened by such an affliction by the providence of God.** It is an offensive hardheartedness that would lead us to be unaffected when the Lord raises His hand to be positioned against us.[24] The psalmist, a man of an excellent spirit, said, "My flesh trembles for fear of You, and I am afraid of Your judgments" (Psalm 119:120). Though a hero may fear the face of no man, he does well to lay aside that bravery of spirit when he faces his God. For this reason, the Lord's anger at David's reproach and threatening dispensation against his child moved him to apply himself to personal fasting and humiliation before the Lord for the life of his child (II Samuel 12:16, 22).

---

[24] Original verbiage: "It is an ungracious hardness, not to be affected when the Lord is lifting up his hand against us."

9. **When one would have clarity and direction about something of particular importance.** It is a sad reality that men who profess to believe in a divine providence over human affairs often take the burden of their matters upon themselves—displaying confidence in their own wisdom, without acknowledging God. This betrays an aim only to please themselves—and not their God—in these matters, as if their desires, convenience, or advantage were the determining factors in their resolutions, rather than their conscience. In such pride, even wise men often make foolish mistakes in their conduct and are left to feel God's just indignation for their rash decisions. Joshua and the princes of Israel, when considering a covenant with the Gibeonites, chose to exercise their judgment and not their faith; vainly imagining they could see well enough with their own eyes, they "took some of their provisions, and did not ask for the counsel of the Lord" (Joshua 9:14). Thus the Gibeonites deviously took advantage of them, as Joshua later realized once it was too late (v.22). We have a divine command and promise that extends both to our temporal and to our spiritual concerns: "Trust in the Lord with all your heart, and lean not on your own understanding; in all your ways acknowledge Him, and He shall direct your paths" (Proverbs 3:5-6 NKJV). This applies directly to our utter dependence as creatures upon God our Creator. We should, therefore, in all things view Him as our **Director**, steering our whole course as He directs by His Word and providence. Since He has promised, "I will instruct you and teach you in the way which you should go [and] will counsel you with My eye upon you" (Psalm 32:8), it is unquestionably our duty to "set the Lord continually" before us (Psalm 16:8). His divine direction must lead us to act or not to act, even as the Israelites in the wilderness went forward or stood still according to whether the pillar of cloud or fire before them went forward or stood still (Numbers 9:15-23). There may be times when a situation does not afford us an opportunity to spend time in solemn prayer, asking God for wisdom; but there is no circumstance that will not permit us to lift our eyes to God and pray a word to Him, requesting His guidance, as Nehemiah did in such a case (Nehemiah 2:4-5).[25] And there is a comforting promise related to these prayers, one that has often been verified in the experience of saints who seek divine direction: "When you walk, your steps will not be impeded; and if you run, you will not stumble" (Proverbs 4:12). Nevertheless, Christians should train themselves to lay their matters before the Lord in solemn prayer for clarity and direction, as much as circumstances allow. Thus Abraham's pious servant did concerning the task his master had committed to him (Genesis 24:12-14). And accordingly he witnessed a wonderful demonstration of the fulfillment of that promise: "When you walk, your steps will not be impeded." And when a matter is considered to be of special magnitude—such as a major life change, an employment decision, some significant venture, or a similar matter—that is a special occasion for a serious Christian to engage in extraordinary prayer with fasting for clarity and wisdom from the Lord, the Father of lights, in order to discover what He is calling him to do. So the captives returning from Babylon with Ezra kept a fast before God at the river Ahava "to seek of Him a right way" (Ezra 8:21 KJV).

10. **When God has provided direction in an important matter, and one must begin to act on that direction.** At such a time, one must recognize his need for God's presence with him if he is to find success in the matter. Thus Esther, when preparing to go before the king to make a request for her people, held a solemn fast with the Jews in Susa (Esther 4:8, 16). And Barnabas and Saul, called by God to a special work, were not sent out until after fasting and prayer (Acts 13:2-3). We need **direction** from the Lord to know our duty in particular cases; once He

---

[25] Original verbiage: "Sometimes, indeed, an affair may be in such a situation, as allows not an opportunity of making an address unto God, for light in it, by solemn prayer; but we are never so circumstanced, but we have access to lift up our eyes to the holy oracle, in a devout ejaculation; as Nehemiah did in such a situation."

has given it, however, we also need His **presence** to go with us, that we might be able to go the way He directs us in righteousness. This is why Moses prayed to God, "If Your presence does not go with us, do not lead us up from here" (Exodus 33:15). Sin defiles everything to us. However promising anything in this world may appear in our eyes, if we do not have the presence of God in it and His purifying blessing upon it, we will find ourselves ensnared by it.

11. **When one is about to encounter some extraordinary difficulty and is in jeopardy of being trapped in sin or in danger.** On such an occasion was the fast at Susa kept; Esther was about to jeopardize her life by going "to the inner court" without being summoned by the king (Esther 4:11, 16). A ship that is sailing in strong wind needs to be well constructed and well balanced; and a Christian who is going through a difficult and ensnaring time has need of prayer and fasting for God's guidance to ensure safe passage through it.[26] Men who trust in themselves in such a case will assuredly find themselves betrayed into snares.

12. **When one desires to approach God with a special solemnity, in which case a special preparation is necessary.** Thus Jacob called his family to prepare themselves when they repented before the Lord at Bethel (Genesis 35:2-3). The Israelites were called to do the same before the solemn occasion of the giving of the Law on Mount Sinai (Exodus 19:10-11, 15). It is also notable that, although the Feast of Booths was the most joyful of all the feasts the Jews celebrated throughout the year, a solemn fast was appointed by God always to be observed before it (Leviticus 23:27, 34). In the method of grace, none are more likely to be lifted up than those who have been most deeply humbled (Isaiah 40:4; Luke 18:14; James 4:10).

With these things in mind, each Christian may be equipped to judge for himself when he is under a providential call to personal fasting and humiliation.

REVIEW QUESTIONS

1. How can fasting be an expression of godly love to our neighbor? How can communion with fellow believers help this endeavor?

_____

_____

_____

_____

_____

_____

---

[26] Original verbiage: "The ship has need to be well ballasted, that sails while the wind blows high; and in a difficult and ensnaring time, there is need of fasting and prayer for Heaven's safe-conduct through it."

2. What are the three general events Boston lists that call for fasting and humiliation? Briefly describe each of them in your own words.

_____

_____

_____

_____

_____

_____

_____

3. Which of the particular cases that Boston describes have you experienced yourself? Are you experiencing any of them currently? According to all you have learned in your study of this discipline, summarize how fasting could be useful or valuable in a specific circumstance that you have faced or are currently facing.

_____

_____

_____

_____

_____

_____

_____

_____

_____

_____

_____

HeartCry Missionary Society at a Glance:

The HeartCry Missionary Society began in 1988 in the country of Peru with a desire to aid indigenous or native missionaries so that they might reach their own peoples and establish biblical churches among them. Since then, the Lord has expanded our borders to include not only Latin America but also Africa, Asia, Eurasia, Europe, the Middle East, and North America.

The goal of our ministry is to facilitate the advancement of indigenous missionaries throughout the world. Our strategy consists of four primary components: financial support, theological training, Scripture and literature distribution, and the supply of any tool necessary to facilitate the completion of the Great Commission.

We currently support approximately 250 missionary families (along with a number of ongoing projects) in over 40 nations around the globe.

Introduction to HeartCry

HeartCry Missionary Society was founded and still exists for the advancement of four major goals:

• The Glory of God
• The Benefit of Man
• The Establishment of Biblical Churches
• The Demonstration of God's Faithfulness

1. The Glory of God

Our first major goal is the glory of God. Our greatest concern is that His Name be great among the nations from the rising to the setting of the sun (Malachi 1:11) and that the Lamb who was slain might receive the full reward for His sufferings (Revelation 7:9-10). We find our great purpose and motivation not in man or his needs but in God Himself; in His commitment to His own glory; and in our God-given desire to see Him worshiped in every nation, tribe, people, and language. We find our great confidence not in the Church's ability to fulfill the Great Commission, but in God's unlimited and unhindered power to accomplish all He has decreed.

2. The Benefit of Man

Our second major goal is the salvation of a lost and dying humanity. The Christian who is truly passionate about the glory of God and confident in His sovereignty will not be unmoved by the billions of people in the world who have "had no news" of the gospel of Jesus Christ (Romans 15:21). If we are truly Christ-like, the lost multitude of humanity will move us to compassion (Matthew 9:36), even to great sorrow and unceasing grief (Romans 9:2). The sincerity of our Christian confession should be questioned if we are not willing to do all within our means to make Christ known among the nations and to endure all things for the sake of God's elect (II Timothy 2:10).

3. The Establishment of Local Churches

Our third major goal is the establishment of biblical churches. While we recognize that the needs of mankind are many and his sufferings are diverse, we believe that they all spring from a common origin: the radical depravity of his heart, his enmity toward God, and his rejection of truth. Therefore, we believe that the greatest possible benefit to mankind comes through the preaching of the gospel and the establishment of local churches that proclaim the full counsel of God's Word and minister according to its commands, precepts, and wisdom. Such a work cannot be accomplished through the arm of the flesh, but only through the supernatural providence of God and the means which He has ordained: biblical preaching, intercessory prayer, sacrificial service, unconditional love, and true Christ-likeness.

4. The Demonstration of God's Faithfulness

The fourth and final goal at HeartCry is to demonstrate to God's people that He is truly able and willing to supply all our needs according to His riches in glory. The needs of this ministry will be obtained through prayer. We will not raise support through self-promotion, prodding, or manipulating our brothers and sisters in Christ. If this ministry is of the Lord, then He will be our Patron. If He is with us, He will direct His people to give, and we will prosper. If He is not with us, we will not and should not succeed. Admittedly, our faith has always been meager and frail throughout the years; but God has always been faithful. As one dear brother puts it: our God delights in vindicating even the smallest confidence of His children.

The Challenge

As Christians, we are called, commissioned, and commanded to lay down our lives so that the gospel might be preached to every creature under heaven. Second only to loving God, this is to be our magnificent obsession. There is no nobler task for which we may give our lives than promoting the glory of God in the redemption of men through the preaching of the gospel of Jesus Christ. If the Christian is truly obedient to the Great Commission, he will give his life either to go down into the mine or to hold the rope for those who go down (William Carey). Either way, the same radical commitment is required.

For more information:

Visit our website at **heartcrymissionary.com** for more information about the ministry—our purpose, beliefs, and methodologies—and extensive information about the missionaries we are privileged to serve.

Printed in Great Britain
by Amazon

36593903R00064